AWK
WRD

We help ministry leaders start social enterprises to sustain themselves long-term so they can seek the betterment of their communities.

AWKWRD: Uncomfortable Conversations in Church Planting That We Avoid

Published by Intrepid. www.intrepidmissions.com

The mission of Intrepid is to elevate marginalized communities and people through training church planters, pastors, and missionaries to start social enterprises to sustain themselves long-term so they can seek the betterment of these overlooked and neglected places and people as they start new churches, businesses, and non-profits.

Intrepid Missions
2034 NE 40th Ave. #414
Portland, OR 97212

Manufactured in the United States of America.

ISBN: 978-0-578-24936-0

CONTENTS

Introduction   1

Chapter 1   7
WHERE DID ALL OF THE LOW-HANGING FRUIT GO?

Chapter 2   13
WHAT GUARANTEES CHURCH PLANTING SUCCESS? YOU
MIGHT BE SURPRISED

Chapter 3   21
CHURCH PLANTERS ARE ALL GOING AFTER THE SAME 5
PERCENT MARKET SHARE … WHY?

Chapter 4   25
DEAR CHURCH PLANTER, IT'S TIME TO PACK YOUR BAGS
AND GO HOME

Chapter 5   31
WHY IS PORTLAND A GRAVEYARD FOR CHURCH PLANTERS?
THAT AND OTHER ABSURDITIES WE TELL IN CHURCH
PLANTING

Chapter 6   37
CHURCH PLANTER, IF YOU REALLY WANT TO BE EFFECTIVE
THEN YOU NEED TO SCRUB YOUR SOCIAL MEDIA

Chapter 7   41
WHY MOST CHURCH PLANTERS I MEET ARE BLOWING IT

Chapter 8   47
MOST CHURCH PLANTS FAIL ... DO YOU WANT TO BE ANOTHER STAT?

Chapter 9   51
WHY MORE CHURCH PLANTERS NEED TO FAIL

Chapter 10   57
WHAT IF THE BEST THING YOU COULD DO WAS FAIL?

Chapter 11   61
LIFE AFTER FAILURE

Chapter 12   65
PERSONAL REFLECTIONS ON THE STATE OF CHURCH PLANTING

Chapter 13   71
RESCUING CHURCH PLANTING FROM SUNDAY MORNINGS

Chapter 14   77
WE'RE GETTING IT ALL WRONG IN CHURCH PLANTING

Chapter 15   81
WHAT CHURCH PLANTING SHOULD LOOK LIKE

Chapter 16   87
SPOILER ALERT: MOST CHURCH PLANTERS ARE NOT VERY ENTREPRENEURIAL

Chapter 17   91
THE MYTHOLOGY OF CALLING

Chapter 18   97
RETHINKING CHURCH PLANTING FUNDING ... NO JOB, NO
FUNDING

Chapter 19   101
THERE'S ONE THING THAT WILL KEEP YOU IN PLACE LONG
TERM AND IT'S NOT A MYSTERY

Chapter 20   105
WHAT YOU'RE MISSING ABOUT BIVOCATIONAL CHURCH
PLANTING

Chapter 21   111
BUT I DON'T WANT TO BE BIVOCATIONAL

Chapter 22   115
SHOULD EVERY CHURCH PLANTER START A SIDE HUSTLE?

Chapter 23   119
CAN YOU REALLY START A CHURCH AND LAUNCH A STARTUP
WITH ZERO MONEY?

Chapter 24   125
WHY SOLO CHURCH PLANTING IS CAREER SUICIDE

Chapter 25   129
HOW DO YOU KNOW WHEN TO GIVE UP YOUR CHURCH
PLANT?

Chapter 26   137
WHAT IF YOUR CHURCH PLANT ISN'T SUSTAINABLE IN 5
YEARS?

Chapter 27   **143**
MOST CHURCH PLANTERS WILL NEED A CAREER OUTSIDE
THEIR CHURCH

Chapter 28   **147**
WHY CURRENT FUNDING MODELS SHORT-CIRCUIT CHURCH
PLANTING

Chapter 29   **151**
"TALK TO ME WHEN YOU'VE RUN OUT OF MONEY"

Chapter 30   **155**
PASTORS ARE CHOOSING THE WRONG PLATFORM: HOW TO
CHOOSE THE RIGHT ONE

Chapter 31   **159**
WHY CHURCH PLANTING IS A HORRIBLE INVESTMENT

Chapter 32   **163**
WHAT YOU NEED TO KNOW ABOUT BIVOCATIONAL CHURCH
PLANTING GOING INTO IT

Chapter 33   **169**
FINDING SUCCESS IN A RESULTS-DRIVEN MINISTRY WORLD

Chapter 34   **173**
WHERE ARE YOU GOING TO PLANT A CHURCH? IN PLACES
YOU WANT OR PLACES OF NEED?

Chapter 35   **179**
MAINSTREAM OR FINGER: WE NEED VOICES FROM THE
MARGINS

Chapter 36   **185**
PLANTING CHURCHES IN A MAJORITY CULTURE SYSTEM

Chapter 37   **191**
WHERE DID THE FRONTIER GO?

Chapter 38   **197**
YOU WILL BE MISUNDERSTOOD

Chapter 39   **201**
CALLING ALL MISFITS

       Bibliography   205
       About the Author   206

x

INTRO

WHY ARE WE AFRAID OF THE TRUTH IN CHURCH PLANTING?

Admittedly I poke a lot when I write. For those who know me know I don't have an axe to grind or anything like that. I just think we get bored with thoughts and ideas, especially when it comes to the mind-numbingly played-out narratives within church planting.

And so I poke ... and prod ... (though not out of angst).

But what is interesting, whether it's from church planters or denominational leaders or national network leaders I receive a lot of feedback. The common response? "Keep writing. Keep saying these things. We need to have these conversations." And so I write ...

The big a-ha moment for me this past year was all of the positive feedback I've received. Something clicked for me in 2020. This was even before the coronavirus hit. I jokingly told my wife that I decided to leave my verbal filter in 2019. No, not in a way that permits me to be a jerk or act inappropriately. Rather, it's the freedom to simply state what is on my mind. Especially in church planting.

I've seen the underbelly of church planting. I don't say that with malice. I'm constantly reminded when I read through the New Testament epistles that from Day One the church was made up of broken people ... redeemed, but broken. I summarize Paul's writings to the churches in various cities as his way of addressing issues that grew out of their struggle with how to follow Jesus. Many had been set free through the good news of a risen Savior and the in-breaking reality of the Kingdom of God. They were struggling to figure out what that meant.

And so Paul told them to ...

Stop gossiping.

Stop sleeping with temple prostitutes.

Stop the orgies.

Stop the divisiveness.

Stop getting drunk during communion.

And if eating meat that had been sacrificed to an idol bothers your conscience then don't eat it. If not, enjoy.

When I read Paul's admonitions I am actually encouraged. Why? Because I see the same stuff happening today in our churches. Maybe we've moved beyond the orgies and are no longer sleeping with temple prostitutes, but we've only replaced them with our own curated list. We have narcissistic celebrity pastors. Materialism. Consumerism. Shady deals and sketchy leadership in the church planting machinery. And so much more.

Why then am I encouraged? Because it's the realization we're flawed and broken, but also redeemed. God continues to do a new work through us. He teaches us dependency on the Holy Spirit to move in and through us despite our frailties and even wanton rebellion. Israel throughout the

Old Testament struggled with this. The church across the pages of the New Testament did as well. We are no different. That's why we had to have things like 99 treatises nailed to a church door.

AWKWRD is not a tell-all exposé on the inside gossip and slander within the church today, and in particular church planting. I wrote it to state the obvious. To have these uncomfortable conversations. Things that church planters struggle with. Messages that denominational and network leaders send to planters that they unwittingly perpetuate. You see, we're all having these conversations. Most often they're in hushed tones in coffee shops with other church planters as we lament together. That's why when I address these topics I constantly get positive feedback … "Keep writing." And so I do.

I address topics we all know to be true but are afraid to mention out loud such as …

Why do white church planters get more money than Hispanic church planters?

Why do church planters avoid low-income communities as a whole and instead plant in hip gentrified neighborhoods or nice suburbs?

Why do most church planters fail (even though we're told otherwise)?

Why is there so much competition in fundraising? Why do we treat it like a game?

Why do church planters succumb to celebrity culture?

Why do good-looking church planters in cool neighborhoods get more funding than not-so-good-looking church planters in uncool neighborhoods?

I could go on and on … and I do. Welcome to the conversation.

AWKWRD

CH 1

WHERE DID ALL OF THE LOW-HANGING FRUIT GO?

It was a transition that hardly anyone noticed. Like a slow gas leak we barely paid any attention to. Then one day we caught a whiff. Like a gas leak. Sneakily and invisibly it has reshaped and reshuffled the landscape of missions and church planting across the United States and Canada (and perhaps other places). What is it? It's the fact that the golden era of church planting is over, at least for this generation. Let me explain.

All of the low-hanging fruit has been picked.

It wasn't too long ago when a church planter could swoop into a city or step out from his staff position at a local megachurch, put on a killer worship service, and poof! Church planting success! Seemingly each city housed a hungry throng of Christians looking for a new church that wasn't like the boring and outdated one they were currently attending or grew up in. So when the new church planter with messed-up hair (or fauxhawk back in the day) rolled into town with a smedium tee and sweet sleeve tats, they gladly jettisoned their church to join this new "innovative," "cutting edge," "relevant" very hip church.

Sadly, those days of easy, fast growth are over. Most of these people are now accounted for. What that means for the church planter rolling into your city (or stepping out from a staff position) is that if he isn't remotely in the Top 10 Cool Pastor list then the likelihood of success is greatly diminished. Of course, my use of "success" is tongue-and-cheek. You probably noticed. I'll circle back around to that later.

I see it all the time. Church Planter A, who might be incredibly cool back home in his rural or suburban setting in the South or Midwest moves to a city like Portland. Back home he was the real deal. He might've had a successful or thriving youth or college ministry. Then he lands in Portland. Within six months he painfully realizes that he may not even crack the Top 25 list at all. He might be lucky to hit the Top 50. As a result, he is four years into his church plant and he has only 25 to 30 people and he feels like a failure.

He was sure a hit back home. But now? He's a small fish in a big pond. But no worries, he has a pocket full of excuses that he pulls out for his donors, denomination, support churches, and last by not least, his own conscience. "This place is just so spiritually dark." "Lost." "They're just not receptive to the gospel." Little does he realize he's peddling excuses for his lack of coolness and charm.

Now let's circle back around to "success" in church planting and why the golden era of church planting is now over. Much of church planting lore has been built on the ability of a church planter to scoop up a throng of Christians interested in something new ... something "fresh." So when 200-500-1,500 worshipping Christians collectively move their attendance and allegiance to this cool new "cutting edge" church that "gets it" we hail it as a success.

The church planter is applauded. He begins speaking at local church planting or denominational gatherings. Soon his fame grows and he's offered regional speaking gigs. Now thanks to social media he decides to begin building his brand. He has a personalized logo. His Instagram is full of photos of him in preaching mode at his church. The lighting hits him just right and the editing in Lightroom is exquisite. He has become the purveyor of thoughtful quotes from his sermons. He now has a book deal and is invited to speak at more and bigger conferences. He's becoming a big deal.

Why? Because he was able to pick the low-hanging fruit. But those days are mostly over.

Sure, on occasion a church planter does pop, even in a city like Portland. When that happens it's usually the same five or seven already existing hip churches who see a decline in attendance (assuming they notice) as people gravitate to the new thing. Like when another coffee shop or brewery opens in Portland. However, we still view that as a success in church planting.

It's time to redefine success.

When did church planting turn into "starting worship services for Christians"? I love J.D. Payne's chapter "Mission and Church Planting" in the book *Theology and Practice of Mission*. He writes, "Biblical church planting is evangelism that results in new churches."[1] That's it. Simple. But that's church planting. OK, if that's church planting, then what do we call these new successful plants that "pop?" I personally don't call them church plants, and I don't mean that as a slight. I simply refer to them as new worship services. Why? Because the process of launching a new worship service is markedly different than creating a new body of believers out of the harvest. It seems the former is par for the course for church planting in the U.S. and the other is reserved for missionaries outside of the U.S. and Canada. Interesting how that works. Semantics.

J.D. doesn't pull any punches when he says:

> Biblical church planting is not about transferring church members from one church to another church. It is not about cloning other "successful" church models into my context. It is not about projecting my culturally preferred way of "doing" church onto a group of new believers, because I "know" best. It is not about starting a new worship service with cool music, great preaching, and meeting in a dark room with a great vibe. Biblical church planting has nothing to do with building a building, stealing another pastor's sheep, or starting a church

---

[1] Payne, "Mission and Church Planting," 203.

simply because my desired "brand" of church is not present in a particular community.[2]

Honestly, I can recall only ever hearing or seeing a handful of churches that actually started through evangelism. (That's over a twenty-year stretch.) You've not heard of them either. Why? Because they mostly came out of addiction centers or the work of minority planters you don't hang out with. Why? Because they're too busy working full-time at their day job so they can lead their church. They don't have time for a mid-morning $4.50 cortado with you.

The golden age of church planting is over. We've had our fun reshuffling sheep and putting on cool events and conferences. Many pastors have made a lucrative career out of this. The golden age may not be completely gone, but it's trending in that direction as most of the low-hanging fruit is now accounted for. I am grateful. This is good news. In fact, this is GREAT news! Why? Because now we can begin to do the work of missionaries and sow the gospel abundantly. As people respond we can gather them together for instruction and worship. As J.D. Payne would say, this is biblical church planting.

---

[2] Ibid.

CH 2

WHAT GUARANTEES CHURCH PLANTING SUCCESS? YOU MIGHT BE SURPRISED

One of my favorite hobbies is to simply observe. It's part of my personality. When I bike all over the city, something I do on a regular basis, I'm always looking at what types of housing are present (mixed use, single-family detached home, etc.), who's on the streets and sidewalks, what's the predominant ethnicity, and more. When I walk into a store I'm always curious as to who is there ... and why? This same trait is at play in church planting. I watch.

Often times that means I watch from afar. I watch church planters come and go. Some make it, but most don't. I see rapid growth, but truth be told most just get by for a few years before they either (a) dig in, get a side job, and decide to stay for the long term, or (b) they close up shop and move on. I'm not here to prop up one choice and deride the other. That's just what I see.

After watching church planting for nearly 20 years I have actually observed a trend that almost always translates into church planting success. Ready? Church planting success inevitably rises and falls on how cool the church planter is.

(Cue the sound of a record scratching.)

Huh?

In other words, the cooler and more hip the church planter is, the better the likelihood of success. Along with that, the stronger and larger their social media presence and platform is, the greater chance of their new church not only making it, but becoming an influencer. In other words, if you're not hip, cool, and even a micro-influencer[1] on social media you're almost dead-in-the-water when

---

[1] Micro-influencers have between 1,000-10,000 followers on social media. Miles, *Instagram Power*, 203.

it comes to church planting and the probability that you'll actually be one who makes it.

You say, would you please unpack that? (I'm glad you asked.)

What I write is influenced by what is currently going on in my life and the culture at large. That's no surprise. When the coronavirus hit resulting in the closure of Sunday worship gatherings I wrote about it and how it intersected with church planting. This morning as I was walking through the manuscript for my book *Intro to the City* I noticed all of the examples and stories of exploring the city with my students from Warner Pacific University plus the insights I gleaned came from learning to see the city from the perspective of people of color. The same applies to this chapter and the backdrop of other teaching and writing projects. In particular, this week I just finished writing the rough draft of my lecture notes for a class on a theology of church planting. Let me explain more.

For the last two months I have spread before me on my desk an array of thick and dense books related to systematic theology, biblical theology, missiology, church planting, and more as I was crafting this course. My mind has constantly been in the mode of thinking about a theology that undergirds church planting. I found that beginning in the Old Testament and all the way through the New Testament, I could trace a theology of church planting. That is to say church planting is not something that started in Acts 2, but instead started much earlier in Genesis 12 with God calling Abram. We can take it one step forward (or backward) and even trace it back to the first few chapters of Genesis and the mission of God. That's been burning in my mind.

Therefore, when I say "What guarantees church planting success? You might be surprised" I'm not even saying I agree with my own observations that the cooler and more hip you are the greater your chances of a church planting success. I tried to develop some theories related to this but I've not found any solid evidence. One study I conducted was about whether church planting success was tied to how many times a church planter rolls his beanie … but the evidence was inconclusive. ;-)

Sure, on one level I can definitely see how church planting success is tied to the appeal, charm, and personal brand of the church planter. But it's the word "success" that I believe we're hung up on. Right? Many church planting networks and denominations have unwittingly defined success as one thing and one thing alone ... numbers. Don't believe me? I have too many stories from too many years sitting in denominational meetings watching leaders decide the future funding of church planters based on the metrics of Sunday worship attendance. We can say it isn't or shouldn't be that way ... and that we value metrics like baptisms, etc., but that really is a smokescreen for the only metric that will keep a planter funded ... numbers (i.e., attendance).

Now back to my class on the theology of church planting. I alluded in the previous chapter to a quote that is worth repeating ... "Biblical church planting is evangelism that results in new churches."[2] Pretty simple and straightforward. Now, let's tie this into what I've been poking and prodding in this chapter about coolness and church planting success. Does coolness relate to success in church planting? Of course, it does. I don't even think that's debatable. However, using the definition above, does that make it "biblical"? No, not at all. It usually looks like this ...

The very cool and coiffed church planter embarks on a church planting journey. Maybe he's a local. Maybe he moves to a new city. But he's

---

[2] Payne, "Mission and Church Planting," 203.

already a big deal ... a ministry influencer (not a micro-, but a macro-influencer).[3] He's going to plant a church. Beginning with interest meetings, working towards a launch means one thing and one thing alone ... he'll attract believers from other churches. No one debates that. So he has a growing core ... all Christians from other local churches. On launch Sunday thanks to his charm, influencer reach, and now a throng of attenders, the church "pops" with 350 people ... 350 people from other churches. This church planter is now well on his way of solidifying his brand as a great influencer, Bible teacher, and aspirational leader. Within three years he has a book deal.

See? Success! I told you what guarantees success. You may not like it, agree with it, or think it should be that way. But according to the system we've set up and the machinery of church planting this is most certainly success. This makes the denomination or church planting network look good. They won't object nor care much where the people came from. It's *their* church plant. *Their* success story.

---

[3] Macro-influencers have between 10,000-100,000 followers on social media. *Instagram Power*, 203.

But what if ... and I am REALLY coloring outside the lines here ... what if new churches were the result of evangelism? I know, a crazy thought. Could we even conceive of such a thing? While it may be biblical church planting, according to our rubric and metrics, that does not translate into a "successful" church plant. So we brush it aside as we hope to find the next emerging ministry influencer.

AWKWRD

CH 3

CHURCH PLANTERS ARE ALL GOING AFTER THE SAME FIVE PERCENT MARKET SHARE ... WHY?

The American church has been planting new churches at an unprecedented clip. While there's much to celebrate in that, unfortunately the parallel storyline isn't such good news. We've made little to no impact. At all. Why? Because somewhere along the way church planters, whether in the city or the burbs or small towns, have collectively gone after the exact same market share. Who are those? (A) Christians from other churches. (B) Unchurched or dechurched Christians. The five percent.

See the problem?

It's all the same market share. Time for a story.

Back in the 1920s only five percent of Americans brushed their teeth on a daily basis. Yes, five percent. The toothpaste manufacturer Pepsodent hired someone who'd become an advertising pioneer ... Claude Hopkins. Hopkins realized that the way to increase sales was not to go after the five percent of tooth-brushers, but the ninety-five percent who did not brush on a daily basis. Through creative marketing those who brushed their teeth daily grew to sixty-five percent within ten years. That is outstanding.

I hope you see where I am going with this. It is rare, and I mean rare, that I find a church planter actually going after the ninety-five percent. Sure, most will claim they are. They're certainly telling their supporters they are. But by perusing their social media ... from the images to the words used ... the overall vibe says ... "Hey, fellow Christians, our church is pretty lit. You should come and check us out. Oh, we have a pourover coffee bar at our Sunday gatherings." #blessed.

However, I don't fault church planters. You have a family to provide for and now a large mortgage or monthly rental in your new city. You know ... and I know … that the only thing your denomination and supporters really care about is how large your Sunday gatherings are … and if they're growing. Are they really interested in you being a missionary? No. Are they much concerned you have a heart for a disenfranchised or left-off-the-radar subculture? No. They simply want a "win." In other words, a good ROI (return on investment). That their missions dollars and offerings led to the establishment of one of their churches in your city. That way in the lobby of their building they can have a map up of the world with all of the thumb tacks showing where they're sending people. It wouldn't look very good to have your thumb tack up only for a few years and then removed because you didn't "make it."

And that is the catch. How will you "make it?" More importantly, how will you make it if you actually went after the ninety-five percent market share that doesn't care (or know) about Christian bands and celebrities or your pourover bar? How do you plant a church among the ninety-five percent? That should be the burning question for all denominations and church planting networks.

Those orbiting Intrepid are those types of planters. They know that reaching the ninety-five percent means rethinking their whole funding model. More than that, it means adopting the lifestyle, identity, and habits of a missionary. That's why they start businesses and non-profits ... to be a blessing, to serve, and to love freely. To live out the gospel in such a way that it sounds like good news when the moments come and you get to share.

This is who I'm throwing my lot in with. The church planting disruptors. Those going after the ninety-five percent.

CH 4

DEAR CHURCH PLANTER, IT'S TIME TO PACK YOUR BAGS AND GO HOME

I have a growing gut-level distaste for seeing church planters roll into a new city and attempting to launch a church from scratch. They're both plucky and naive. They pour everything into their dream of their new church "popping" ... only to see them go back home disappointed a few years later because it didn't pan out. Is it even worth it? I'm now more than ever convinced of this ... would-be church planters should just stay home.

OK, if you've been following along for any length of time you know I'm trying to press a point.

Yes, I'm using hyperbole. Kind of. Sort of. Maybe a little, but not as much as you'd think. I know I sound like a broken record when I write things like, "I've been watching church planting going on for almost 20 years now." That's not that much time. However, that's enough time to at least begin noting and observing patterns. When it comes to this conversation the pattern I see most vividly is that most often the best church planters are actually locals.

I've been around long enough now to see the typical church planting storyline. I'll tell this story using the not-so-fictitious characters of Church Planter A and Church Planter B. Are you ready? This may sound familiar as I've been writing a lot about this lately.

Church Planter A moves from Houston, Dallas, Nashville, or from a small town in the Midwest. His denomination or network is desperate to get a foothold in a certain city. Not just the metro area, but the city. Not just within the city limits, but the urban core. So Church Planter A, with his family in tow, lands in one of the city center's trendy neighborhoods. Within months comes the horrific realization … not only are there four-to-five other church planters in the same neighborhood, but some of the most well-known and highly regarded "hipster" churches are also there.

The painful reality is Church Planter A is not nearly as cool as the pastor of the highly regarded hipster church (who's also from that city or region). Any hope of snagging the low-hanging fruit of young adults looking for a church is gone. All of those people have already been swept up into a myriad of hip churches. As a result, after three-to-five years, if Church Planter A had launched a worship gathering, it is small, unassuming, and not the ticket to financial independence that he had hoped for.

Church Planter A then has a couple of options: (1) stick it out and plead with donors for "one more year," (2) get a part-time job and settle in for the long-term, or (3) polish off his resume and look for a ministry gig elsewhere.

Let's look at Church Planter B's story to see the difference. Church Planter B feels burdened for his community. He knows the people. He loves the people. He has a history with the people. Why? Because he's local. They grew together. With a strong relational network in place, he ventured out to plant a church. Maybe he had been on staff at a church or came out of a campus ministry background. Sure enough, he's running hard in the church planting endeavor.

Like Church Planter A, he too faces the reality that most of the accounted-for unchurched and dechurched in his city and region have been swept up by other church plants. But Church Planter B knows this isn't a sprint. Besides, where does he need to rush off to? So his church bumps along. No, it didn't explode like he'd hoped. But for him part-time or bivocational church planting is non-negotiable. It was built into his DNA from even before he began. Why? Because he's already home.

When Church Planter A runs into obstacles or barriers, there's always the option of "going home." But for Church Planter B, he's already there because he never left. In other words, he's already planning for the long-term. If that means working part-time, then it's a no-brainer.

See the difference? Looking back over nearly twenty years I saw this same trend play out in every city I've lived in. Most often the best church planters are local. Is this always the case? No, not at all. Does this mean a church planter shouldn't move to a new city to plant? No, not at all. I'm just pointing out trends I've seen. Trends reflect the overarching curve, not the unique storyline of each and every person.

I would be remiss if I didn't point out one more key difference. I've alluded to it already. Church Planter B knows the people ... loves the people ... is deeply burdened for the people. So often in talking with Church Planter A, I hear a hype and excitement about church planting. But in conversations with Church Planter B, all I hear them talk about is people. Again, see the difference? One loves the prospect of church planting. The other loves the people.

I'd like to point out that we've been doing this for centuries in mission fields, right? Outside missionaries move in, evangelize, start a church, raise up locals, and build their leadership base with these locals. The end goal? To make this an indigenous movement spearheaded by locals whereas the outsiders move on to help catalyze a movement elsewhere. That's also what we see Paul doing in the New Testament as well. He was never primarily a pastor. He evangelized in a city, planted a church community, raised up leaders, and moved on.

Obviously, there's A LOT more to this conversation than there is time or space to cover in this chapter. My goal was to simply poke a stick through the spokes of your front tire.

What if we had more Church Planter B's? In case you're wondering ... I know all about Church Planters A's because I was Church Planter A several times over.

CH 5

WHY IS PORTLAND A GRAVEYARD FOR CHURCH PLANTERS? THAT AND OTHER ABSURDITIES WE TELL IN CHURCH PLANTING

If I had a nickel for every time someone said "Portland is a graveyard for church planters" I'd be a millionaire. It's just simply not true. It has become one of those statements that gets repeated enough times that people believe it is actually true (and because no one knows the source). Most often church planters are told this before they move here. Maybe to them it just adds to Portland's allure. But it's not just Portland. I've heard the same descriptor applied to Chicago, New York, Seattle, Boston, and every other church planting hotspot. So what's the real story behind it all?

I've shared this before, but on any given week I ride roughly 100 miles around the city of Portland. I'm constantly exploring and getting exercise while I'm at it. Over the years my explorations have covered different parts of the city and surrounding suburbs. For the last year or so most of my journeys have taken me into the hinterlands of Portland. Or what I call "the other Portland." Most outsiders think of our city as full of left-leaning white hipsters sipping on $4.50 cortados during the day in a coffee shop while working on a marketing campaign for Nike. That really only represents a small slice of Portland. I call that the *Portlandia* Portland.

For some reason almost all the church planters I meet say they're "called" to reach *Portlandia* Portland. What about the rest of Portland beyond the city center? If most church planters are opting for the *Portlandia* Portland they're in for a rude awakening. It's already saturated with church planters and large vibrant churches in the urban core. I watch as church planter after church planter move to Portland all targeting the same demographic that these larger churches are already connecting with. However, most church planters are not nearly as cool as the lead pastors of these churches. Also, these churches have great reputations (among other Christians). As a result, whenever Christians move into the city from outside Portland they'll more than likely land in one of these churches. The lone church planter, who might've been a big deal back home in his small city, is not going to cut it here. And so the storyline goes ...

Sure, the newly arrived plucky church planter will inevitably get the leftovers from these influential churches. These are usually people who've left those churches because they're not happy ... "The church is too big." "We don't know the pastor. He's too inaccessible." "We just want a small church." Then they come over to the new church. You're excited. They even tithe. Then after a year these people realize you're just not as cool or they're frustrated with the low quality of your services, music, and programs. And so they migrate back to the mothership.

This is why and how Portland has earned the reputation of being a graveyard for church planters. It's true ... because most church planters are all targeting the same churched demographic that are already being swept up into growing, healthy, and vibrant city center churches. Church planters cannot seem to pry these people away from their churches to come to theirs. Oh, but the new church planter will continue to send newsletters back home telling everyone just how difficult it is and will probably remind his supporters at least once a year that Portland is a graveyard for church planters.

Back to my bike ride.

Whenever my bike rides take me to the hinterlands I keep thinking to myself, "Why don't more church planters come out here?" I mean, you won't be bumping up against other church planters. Also, it's a world away from where the people live who populate these large city center churches. "Out there" ... but still inside the city limits ... is waiting. I'm not saying there are no incredible churches there already. It's just that they just don't get the fanfare that these other big churches do.

As I said, this is not simply a Portland phenomenon. Every city has what I call these hinterlands. These are off-the-map places and people that rarely get the attention of church planters and their respective denominations or networks.

This also brings up another painful reality ... we need more non-white church planters. On one level, it makes sense for white church planters to target white populations in the same way Hispanic church planters reach other Hispanics. That probably explains why in Portland once you leave the city center there are fewer church planters. You see, these areas are more non-white. I see it every day on my bike rides. So what point (or points) am I trying to make?

Portland is only a "graveyard" because church planters tend to cluster in the same over-saturated parts of the city where there are not only many other church plants, but also a throng of growing and heathy larger churches.

Hinterlands are overlooked. They're not cool or trendy. And if most church planters are white then we have a problem.

Many of these hinterlands are lower income, regardless of ethnicity. Therefore, church planters need a different funding model because these churches may never become "self-sustaining" in the traditional sense of how church plants are funded after five years.

So what am I really saying? I'm a fan of hyperbole and anecdotes. Why? Because I like to think of myself emulating Jesus ("It is easier for a camel to go through the eye of a needle than for a rich person to enter the kingdom of God"). I'm not cranky. I'm actually a huge fan of church planters everywhere.

When it comes to cities like Portland being some horrific graveyard for church planters? It's simply not true. Church planters (mostly white) are just all planting in the same part of the city targeting the same demographic ... young, white, Christian. To me that's a far cry from church planting being the missionary endeavor that it is supposed to be. That proposition is for the long term ... ten-to-twenty years. Those churches may never be self-sustaining. But nor should that be the focus. Instead, let's opt for the hinterlands.

CH 6

CHURCH PLANTER, IF YOU REALLY WANT TO BE EFFECTIVE THEN YOU NEED TO SCRUB YOUR SOCIAL MEDIA

Who are you? How do you self-identify? The answers to those questions are revealing. Why? Because it's about our personal identity. Yet we know that it's not so cut-and-dry. There's you … and then there's the "social media you." Which one is true?

This is especially relevant for church planters and others in "professional" ministry. How do you self-identify on social media? Are you known as the "church" guy or gal? What does the bulk of your posting and interaction reveal on social media? Is it mostly ministry-related? If so, who do you assume is following and interacting with you? Probably others who are just like you. Other ministry professionals.

The follow up question then is … are you happy with that? Is that what you want? I've heard from many who say, "I use such-and-such platform for peer ministry connections." I get that. However, do you also know that these are also public forums? Meaning, while you may think all you're doing is having "in-house" conversations you're doing so publicly.

Think about it. You've done it … I've done it … when you first meet someone one of the first things you do is find them on social media. You want to get a feel for who they are, what they're about, etc. I can guarantee people are doing that to you … and me. Therefore, what should our social media be about?

I'm not against you always posting Bible verses, churchy things, sermon series, in-house Christian things, retweets from your ministry hero, etc. But be aware that your social media is really your personal brand. Let me put it like this … you're a brand. What that means is everything you communicate reveals a value system … your value system. It tells others what your "brand" is. So it does make sense for you to post churchy things. However, here's the rub, what that means though is that 99.87543% of those who follow you are just like you. Therefore anything and everything you do and broadcast is to those who are already your "in-crowd."

You have 2 choices:

1. Continue on in the same way.
2. Scrub your social media. (I said, scrub, NOT delete)

Wait, what?

See, it goes back to identity and how you self-identity. Are you a religious professional (church planter, ministry leader, missionary, etc)? If you were moving to Dubai, Moscow, Dublin, or Beijing how would you self-identity? How would you utilize social media?

Maybe it's time to scrub your social media. No, you're not ashamed of the gospel or anything like that. You're just being a good missionary. But if your goal and aspiration is to be a great Christian thought leader and influencer then you should probably keep doing what you're doing.

CH 7

WHY MOST CHURCH PLANTERS I MEET ARE BLOWING IT

Too often the words we use can become so commonplace that they lose their potency. For years we've talked so much about being missional or incarnational that those words have become simply a backdrop. Worse yet, they are niceties to put on websites or the church planting prospectus we cobbled together to raise funds. Sometimes it takes stepping out of our own circles to see what we've been missing. That's what happened to me last week.

It changed everything.

Admittedly, as some of you know, I no longer read the latest buzz in ministry or church planting. Neither articles nor books. Twelve years ago I stopped. Sure, once in a while I do but today I spend the bulk of my time reading about marketing, urban studies, branding, social media, travel, community development, business, and more. Most of it is tied to courses I'm teaching or for our Intrepid coaching. But what continually stands out is when I read things that have direct correlation to ministry. I stop, put the book down, look out the window, and reflect on it. My follow-up thought is always, "How do I bring this into church planting?"

I've started reading the book *Hook Point: How to Stand Out in a 3-Second World* by Brendan Kane. I came across this book because we use Kane's *One Million Followers: How I Built a Massive Social Following in 30 Days* for our startup coaching. I'm also using it next semester for a university course I'm teaching on social media and analytics. For all of the church planters in our coaching looking to start businesses and non-profits these books have been great resources. What caught my attention was in the foreword to *Hook Point*.

The foreword writer (Vishen Lakhiani, founder of Mindvalley) was talking about how to better communicate with potential audience members and customers (which *Hook Point* is about) when he dropped four nuggets that stopped me in my tracks. While he was speaking to entrepreneurs what he said I knew immediately also applied to church planters. In particular, his second point is a fresh take on the tired and played-out term incarnational: *Become your demographic.*

That's it! That is one of the clearest delineations I see among church planters. That also is the difference between those who "get it" and those who're "blowing it." Most church planters I meet are doing ministry from a distance … at arm's length. They're outsiders. Not one of "us." They are the "them." All they want to do is make a splash on social media, lock in a cool venue for worship services, and go big on launch Sunday … and then … POOF … off to the races.

Wait, I take it back. Most church planters I meet are actually insiders … they are their demographic. Meaning a subcultural group of Christians. That's why their church plant draws nearly a 100 percent hit rate from other Christians. Then they wonder why no one else comes. Also, we know that when other Christians hop onto the new, cool, and hip church they're also bringing with them their expectations from their previous churches. If they decide you don't measure up then they'll give you an earful before bailing on you for an even fresher and more hip new church.

You've been played.

That's because you are your demographic. But you're going after the wrong demographic.

Were you called to move across the country and spend hundreds of thousands of support dollars just so you can snag Christians from other churches? What's the solution?

Become your demographic.

What that may mean is you need to find a new demographic. If you did, which would you choose?

We talk the talk of being incarnational but I'm afraid it simply is a nicety that we brandish to look like we're "in the know" in ministry. What if you stepped out of your demographic and into a whole new one? One where you're surrounded by people who don't identify with Christ?

I'm afraid that unless we do this we'll continue to plant churches for area Christians and then wonder why we're not connecting with everyone else in our city. In Portland we talk about how it's crowded in church planting. It certainly is ... since most church planters are going after the same

Christian demographic. But I would point out that ninety-plus percent of the city could care less about whether or not you have a pourover bar at your worship services or about a logo you spent too much money on.

What would it look like to become your demographic?

AWKWRD

CH 8

MOST CHURCH PLANTS FAIL ... DO YOU WANT TO BE ANOTHER STAT?

Everything comes with risk. There are no guarantees. That transcends all areas of life and work. However, we also know that there are pathways that ensure a greater likelihood of success. Take university degrees for example. You're more apt to immediately find a job after graduation if your degree is in nursing compared to history, philosophy, or that glorious "general studies" degree. The same principle applies in church planting.

If you've tracked along with Intrepid for any length of time you know I cite often the phrase "most church plants fail." It's true. Painfully true. Now what you're probably looking for is more granular data. Which ones fail? Which ones make it? How much does geography influence a church plant's survivability? Also, what about the other factors like assessment, training, funding, coaching, or ethnicity? Here's what I know … most church plants I've observed going on twenty years have failed … stopped … ceased to exist. Sure, some fold within four years while others after eight. But looking back over this time period I'm hard-pressed to find ones that actually made it.

If that's true, then why do it? Why go into church planting? Or is it like the college degree conversation? Obviously everything and anything is risky, right? But a degree in nursing lines you up to seamlessly slide into work at a hospital or clinic immediately after graduation (same with teachers) whereas the philosophy major is probably talking your ear off as he pours your latte at the local coffee shop he works at. Fair assessment? Probably not, but you get the point.

What if there was a way to safeguard against failure in church planting? No, it's not foolproof. Consider it an alternative pathway.

I'm not talking about getting more donors and support churches. All that does is drag out the inevitable if you don't have a sustainable model. Dependency on outside donors is not a sustainable model unless you're doing so in the same manner as a career missionary who raises funds for the long-term. But most church planters assume their plant will be self-sustaining after five years which means their funding eventually runs out and their sponsors are nowhere near able to support them. But you already know this, especially if you've been following along.

So what is this mythical pathway I speak of? Start a business. Launch a non-profit.

Wait, doesn't that sound like the student who's double majoring in philosophy AND history? "Can I get three shots of espresso instead of two in my latte?" you ask your college-educated barista with a double major.

Again, everything comes with risk. There are no guarantees. Actually the best guarantee is to not leave your sweet job or cushy lesser role on staff at a big church. But you don't want to. You can't. You must plant. You feel like God has called and compelled you. Good. We're in agreement. But don't you want to at least give yourself a better shot of actually making it? There's nothing worse than going to supporting churches, denominations, and donors and say, "Hey y'all, it's been a fun ride, but our church never really got past thirty-five people (fifty-two with kids, mind you) in six years. I just got a job on staff at my buddy's church so the $650,000 that you all kicked in for me to plant the church ... well, it didn't quite pan out. Thanks for the memories!" Yeah, no.

It is true that here at Intrepid we focus on helping church planters (and pastors, ministry leaders, and missionaries) launch a social enterprise ... a business or non-profit. Is this the only way? No, not at all. It's one way among many. An alternative pathway. I just want to see you succeed and stay where you're planting long term. I know how painful it is to not succeed. You feel like you let everyone down, God included. But it doesn't have to be this way. There are other viable pathways and I adamantly believe that launching a business or non-profit is the equivalent of nudging you towards getting that nursing degree instead of philosophy. Besides, as a nurse you can still read your books from obscure writers on some nuanced and niche 18th-century philosophical construct.

CH 9

WHY MORE CHURCH PLANTERS NEED TO FAIL

Failure. The word haunts us. We avoid it like that cooked salmon that has been sitting in the back of the refrigerator for over a week. We melt when we think of having that label applied to us. Failure.

Why do we have such an obsession with failure? Why is it the very last thing that we ever want to do? Each semester, at the beginning of every class I teach when we do those awkward introductions that everyone hates I have students share: (1) Who are you? (2) Where are you from? (3) Why are you here? (3) What do you hope to get out of this course? (4) What excites you about this course? (5) What makes you nervous about this course? (6) What is something you're afraid of? When it comes to answering that last question students usually steer off in one of two directions. (a) They share something funny … "I'm afraid of spiders." We all laugh. There's usually a story. Or (b) students flip the serious switch on. The question is usually answered in this way … "I'm afraid of failure."

Why?

Just so you don't assume that I've moved beyond fear-of-failure I'm right there with you. Fear of failure rears its ugly head in my life as well. But what if? What if we actually embraced it? You see, the very thing that we're most afraid of can actually be the greatest gift we'll receive in our lives. We need to fail. Fall flat on our faces. Suck. Bomb. Flame out. Implode.

Obviously, I'm not talking about moral failure or anything like that. Simply put: we need to fail … and fail often. For some reason in life and in particular in ministry we're not allowed to fail. I get it. We wrap our identity and self-worth in what we do. Then we add the extra layer of "God called me to this" which totally ramps up failure anxieties. What if I fail? What will people think? I told everyone God called me to this. Did I let him down?

The best thing a church planter can do is fail. Why? Because the next time you plant (and there *should* be a next time) you'll know better what to do and what not to do. Interestingly, I was reading a textbook on, of all topics, social media analytics when I came across this quote:

> If you're thinking about doing something, and you're worried about doing it, ... ask yourself a simple question: Is what I'm about to do going to land me in jail? Is it going to cause an international incident? Or, am I going to be homeless? ... The worst that happens is you fail, and you try again, and as long as you learn something from the failure, I don't consider it a failure. I will never hire anyone who has not failed. I want you guys to fail. I want you to fail so hard that it blows your mind. You can't imagine. Trust me when I say this, if you continue down the entrepreneurial path, you have no clue right now, how hard you're going to fail ... It's going to be awesome ... because every time I've failed, and I've failed a ton, I learn so much.[1]

What if ... what if we had that same mindset in church planting? Would there be more people signing up to fail? I hope so. We already know that

1 Lipschultz, *Social Media Measurement and Management*, 199.

most church plants fail in the same way that most business startups don't succeed either. Rather than being paralyzed by it, what if we embraced it?

In skateboarding it's called progression. You progress daily by your failures. Overcome and unlock that new trick. It takes repetition.

But the irony is that this is one of those things we don't talk about going into church planting. What if during your assessment and training you heard, "Listen, most of you will fail. Don't sweat it. Don't be paralyzed by the moment. Don't work towards perfection. Take risks. Be bold. Don't wrap your identity into this. Who knows, maybe by your fourth church plant you'll get it all figured out. Go for it!"

Sadly, we don't talk that way. If you fail, your denomination will be out financially, it'll be hard to get your donors back onboard for "one more try," and in ministry circles you may garner the reputation of "that dude who failed." But who cares? Seriously, who really cares?

We've so mythologized "calling" that we forget to realize that most of those God called throughout Scripture suffered greatly. Even failed by our standards. Things didn't go well. Hosea married a prostitute. Moses messed up and couldn't enter the promised land. Jeremiah … poor guy. Paul was routinely beaten and imprisoned. You get the point. What was the cost of their obedience? Did God guarantee them great ministry stature and a huge following on social media? Were they promised to be the next ministry social media influencer? No, they just did what they were told. The results weren't even up to them anyways.

Church planter … I want you to fail. And when you do you need to get back up and try it again … and again … and again. You have nothing to lose. If the King of the Universe tells you he loves you then who cares what anyone else thinks?

CH 10

WHAT IF THE BEST THING YOU COULD DO AS A CHURCH PLANTER WAS FAIL?

Continuing on in the failure conversion … as I just wrote in the previous chapter, no one wants to be a failure. But I want more people to fail.

So why do I wish for every church planter to fail?

It's simple. So they will quickly realize that what they're doing and how they're going about it does not work. I can talk with church planters until I'm blue in the face about thinking long-term, creating alternative income streams, and launching social enterprises that not only sustains them but seeks the betterment of their communities and is their platform for ministry. But the funded church planters will simply opt to keep going until they've blown through the money they've raised. If they don't completely up and leave, they may come around and talk to me.

I'm not being mean-spirited. I just know that the typical church planter is not only naive but is dripping with hubris and ego. No one will tell them what to do, especially those who've raised a lot of funds. They seem to think that because they can raise funds that will translate into successfully planting a growing church. Unfortunately, both of those are two completely different skill sets.

So hurry up and fail, run out of money, and then come talk to me before it's too late.

Now, does that sound like hubris and ego on my part? Possibly. However, I know the typical church planter because I was that church planter. I listened to the wooing of my denomination, thought they had my best interests in mind, sold the farm, and plunged headlong into planting "my way." But my way didn't work. It rarely does.

So I had to fail. Not just once, but repeatedly. I was and am stubborn.

But interestingly, it was through my failure and coming to the end of myself that I found true freedom and momentum in ministry. I now share the gospel and disciple people towards maturity in Christ more than I ever did as a marginally-funded church planter. I also don't have those pesky monthly reports to fill out where I let my denomination know how many people I baptized, how many times I shared my faith, how many Bible studies I started, and so on. I now minister from a place where I want to be and not because my funding is dependent on it.

Besides, I've been there. My denomination cut my funding eighteen months into a church plant because I wasn't progressing fast enough. The longer I'm in this the more I hear similar stories from church planters all over the country.

I decided to no longer play the game.

I know many other planters who are in the same boat. It is at this crossroads one of two things usually happens. Many (most?) will not only jettison their church plant, but walk away from ministry altogether. I don't blame them. I was on that same trajectory. I sat in PhD classes on urban planning determined to kick any idea of ministry to the curb and get a sweet gig as a university professor reading obscure academic journals. Now, I'm not saying that's a wrong or bad path. Lots of amazing ministry can happen in those settings because it happens all the time. It just wasn't for me at that moment.

The second alternative is to find a more sustainable model of ministry. One that is not predicated on "fruit" or appeasing donors and supporters by falsifying stats (yes, church planters do this ALL OF THE TIME). I'm 100 percent onboard with communicating to donors, supporters, etc., but not out of fear of losing my funding.

That's why you need to create a different income stream. For some that's in the form of getting a job. I know many church planters who not only did that, but did so in order to keep at church planting. Kudos and props! For others, and this ties into what I do through Intrepid, failure opens the door to consider an alternative pathway of launching a business or non-profit. Agreed, it's not for everyone. However, it's for a lot more than you realize.

CH 11

LIFE AFTER FAILURE

This is a question I've been thinking about more and more over the past few years. I've known a lot of church planters over the years … A LOT. However, most are no longer planting. Where did they all go? Maybe, the better question is … what did we all end up doing after our church planting failure?

But what is "failure" in church planting? Is it really that cut and dry? The new church either took root and grew (and maybe multiplied) or the seed never took root. Is it failure if our role is simply to plant and water since God brings the growth? We can have that conversation at another time. For now

I'm more interested in what everyone is doing in life after their church plants never took root.

This conversation has me thinking about conducting some kind of research project. Since most church plants don't take root wouldn't it be helpful to note and pay attention to where former church planters end up? Besides carrying an inordinate amount of inner guilt that they didn't "make it," I wonder where we all ended up.

Notice I said "we." I'm the product of three … yes, three … church plants that never took root long-term. The first time around I handed off the lead role after two years in order to step into a denominational role. The plant lasted another eight years before merging with another church. The second time was when we had our funding cut since we weren't progressing fast enough. By the third time I had lost my stomach for it and about two years in I simply stopped (we weren't meeting publicly yet). In other words, I know a thing or two about what happens when new churches don't take root.

Since I was bivocational from the get-go in church planting I never wrestled with "getting a job" outside of ministry. As I've written about and shared before, I've found more ministry opportunities outside of paid ministry. It's not that I am pitting one against the other, but I've long since jettisoned this notion of "ministry" versus "secular" work outside of ministry. Most of what I do never shows up on social media … nor should it … nor do I even do it to broadcast on a public forum. Is this the fate of "failed" church planters?

Do most failed church planters (also insert: pastors, missionaries, other ministry leaders, etc.) simply slide into new jobs and careers with little to no fanfare? They take up jobs as teachers, business owners, entrepreneurs, tech workers, realtors, selling insurance, and so much more. I'm not as much concerned with what anyone does post-church planting, but my curiosity lies in the "why?" Why did you choose this new career path? Did you simply have your taste of ministry and it left a bad taste in your mouth? Was there irreparable damage to your own soul, psyche, well-being, and family?

One of the common narratives I actually do hear way too often is a feeling of a sense of letdown and betrayal. I've heard over and over former church planters share how their denominations let them down, didn't care for them, and ultimately simply cast them aside for the next round of church planters moving to their city. In other words, they were left and forgotten. So it made sense to slide into a new career. Every city is filled with former church planters, pastors, and missionaries who're doing other things that have nothing to do with paid ministry.

Young church planter, before you dismiss this, I'd like to point out that this is more of a norm than an anomaly. In other words, most likely your new church won't make it ... assuming you're operating on conventional church planting funding. Sure, a few actually "make it" but most don't. Are you ... or can you ... plan for life after planting? What would it look like? What would you do?

This is why I'm so passionate about helping church planters, pastors, missionaries, and ministry leaders launch startups. Why? To offer you a different funding model that gives you a better chance for long-term sustainability while beginning to build a career outside of paid ministry that is not predicated on church growth. Why? So you can actually make the choice and decide for yourself how long you want to stay in it rather than being forced out by your funding either getting cut off or eventually running out. If it is any encouragement, this is what we saw Paul do throughout his ministry. He worked outside of "paid ministry" so he could be freed up to do ministry long-term.

CH 12

PERSONAL REFLECTIONS ON THE STATE OF CHURCH PLANTING

Admittedly, I'm not the most expressive person. According to a variety of personality tests I'm a high introvert … even off the charts. I'm a 5w4 on the Enneagram. I value alone time, down time, and reflection. Sometimes I prefer books, writing, and ideas more than being with people. As a result, I fail to realize that at times I come across a certain way. Given over to the extremes of my personality I can even be considered aloof.

So why bring this up?

Pity? Sympathy? Empathy? No, once in a while I feel this strong compulsion to pause, pull back the curtains and let you inside for a moment. Just a moment. There are times in a conversation with someone when I see how I've either miscommunicated or under-communicated. (I'm also hyper-aware since I teach Interpersonal Communication every semester to undergrads). That has prompted me to "pen" a manifesto of sorts. Well, maybe not quite a manifesto, but more like personal reflections on church planting. In the midst of constantly reading, writing, and teaching I am briefly hitting the pause button to hopefully be able to articulate where I am at in regards to church planting and what it means for Intrepid.

Why?

Because I fear that I can box myself in. I'm for *this* kind of church planting … and against *that* kind of church planting? Is that what I mean? I thought it'd be helpful for those of you who're either involved with Intrepid or somewhere orbiting our faint gravitational pull to clarify. Ready? Here we go …

I believe in church planting … all kinds of church planting. I don't think there's one way to plant a church. I'm honestly a fan of all … attractional, seeker, organic or simple or house, legacy or traditional, and everything in between. One of the richest ministry experiences I have ever had was as an interim pastor at an established church. I saw God work and move in ways that dumbfounded me as I was coming off the heels of several iterations of house-church planting. The gathered church always reflects the prevalent culture of those who make up the church and the surrounding community.

I don't think bivocational / covocational church planting is the only way. Seriously. Not everyone should plant this way. While it is more normative for the Two-Thirds world, full-time ministry is a luxury in Western cultures. Pastors and church planters can actually choose to be bivo or not. I won't fault anyone who chooses not to go the bivocational route. Given the professionalism of church planting today and the common storyline of how most church planting happens in the U.S. I can see why the bivo approach isn't for everyone. You know where Intrepid and I lean strongly in this conversation, but at the end of the day I'm simply for church planting. Period.

While site selection in church planting is a passion of mine, I won't fault a church planter from planting in a desirable place. Even though it was almost difficult to type that sentence I still believe it. I have so many friends and acquaintances who're planting in the cool and trendy kinds of places that I regularly push back against. But I don't push back because I don't believe we should plant churches there. I even remind these friends that I'm all for them and their church planting efforts. While I'm an advocate for marginalized people and off-the-beaten-path kinds of places I still celebrate whenever and wherever churches are being planted.

Intrepid isn't the only or best way. Those who're grabbing onto Intrepid and our coaching are doing so for a reason ... it resonates. It meets a need for a certain breed of church planters, pastors, missionaries, and social entrepreneurs. I suppose that means we're niche. I'm actually good with that. This kind of church planting (church planting + community development + social entrepreneurship) isn't for everyone. As a result, I'm looking to run fast with those who're already moving in this direction. Even yesterday in one of our coaching calls I was so encouraged and humbled to hear church planters talk about their heart's desire to start businesses, create jobs, and seek the betterment of their communities through economic development with the same gusto and passion as seeing a new church birthed and helping people walk towards Jesus. The truth is, it's not either/or but both/and. I am proud of what we're building with Intrepid.

Four points. That suffices. Again, I simply wanted to seek to clarify some things. No, I've not had people yelling at me or pushing back. Since it's easy to live inside my own head I want to also ensure I continually repeat these points. While I do that often in our coaching unless you're in one you probably won't hear it much. This is for you to know where I'm coming from.

Thanks for following along.

AWKWRD

CH 13

RESCUING CHURCH PLANTING FROM SUNDAY MORNINGS

If you've recently started orbiting around Intrepid you may have lingering thoughts, questions, and even concerns. Right? For example ... are we advocating a certain style, mode, or model of church? Given the various topics that we intentionally push back on are we against the "system" of church planting? Also ... what's up with the title of this chapter? Are we against Sunday gatherings for worship, teaching, and celebration? Now let me unpack this ...

We can all agree that different influences shape our lives which spill over into our identity. What we do influences who we are. We spend an inordinate amount of time in that arena. Most notably our jobs, careers, occupations, or vocations. For the past nearly twenty years one of the defining influences in my life has been church planting. I have been a church planter and worked with countless planters over the years in various roles and responsibilities. I'm a huge fan and advocate of church planting. I still brandish the label "church planter." Proud of it too.

But there's a catch. Right? That's what you were waiting for. Here it is ...

We need to rescue church planting from Sunday mornings. The older I get the more perspective I gain. No, not because I'm drawing from a secret well of wisdom. Like you, I've seen a lot. The longer we're into something the more we see. So what have I seen? MOST who venture into church planting are seven-to-ten-to-fifteen years later no longer church planting ... or for that matter in any intentional ministry role whether paid or not. After having been bruised and battered they slide into another career ... business startups, teaching, investments, real estate, whatever.

So why do most church planters "fail?"

Notice I put "fail" in quotation marks because I rarely (if at all) would ever say that anyone has ever failed at church planting. What I mean is this ... they were not successful enough in gathering a growing group of people on Sundays who'd eventually (sooner, not later) tithe enough so the church planter could sustain his livelihood and family. THAT IS THE PRIMARY DETERMINING FACTOR OF WHETHER A CHURCH PLANTER STAYS OR GOES. I wasn't very good at that either.

That line of reasoning always causes tension within me ... and I mean A LOT. No, not tension about the need for church planters to earn and sustain a livelihood. It instead comes from the means or methods from which that livelihood is derived and all of the ensuing challenges that go with it. The New Testament is not helpful if you're looking for a clear-cut model of sustainability for church planters / missionaries / pastors. We see clear indicators that it is right for church planters (or pastors or missionaries) to be compensated by their churches. But also see clear indicators where Paul eschewed that right so as to not be a burden to the church. Therefore my question is ... when did church planting become about Sunday mornings?

Let's play a word association game,. Ready? When I say "church planter" what comes to mind? Sundays, right? Don't believe me? (A) That's how church planters are measured. (B) A growing Sunday gathering is really the only indicator of whether denominations, networks, and supporters will continue to fund a church plant. (C) That, as I mentioned above, makes it the PRIMARY indicator of "success" or "failure." And then my follow-up question is … since when did church planting cease to become a missionary endeavor?

It is on that question that I want to land this chapter. Since when did your ability to grab Christians from a variety of local churches into your new church become the hallmark of church planting success? At what point did the work of establishing new churches shift from a missionary venture to how awesome your Sunday experience is … whether in-person or online or both?

Those questions haunt me. Do they haunt you? But since we've predicated success and failure on a church planter's ability to grow a Sunday gathering then WHY WOULD THEY NOT TRY TO GROW IT AT ALL COSTS? That is code for "hoping 'solid' Christians from other churches will shift their allegiances over to you and your new church."

Right? If you don't believe me then you're not aware of what really happens in church planting.

Church planting needs to be rescued from Sunday mornings. It also needs to be taken out of the hands of pastors and preachers and put back where it belongs … into the hands of missionaries. That is my slant, my angle on church planting for Intrepid. That's why I believe strongly in helping church planters launch social enterprises to (A) sustain themselves long-term and (B) seek the betterment of the communities they are in.

AWKRD

CH 14

WE'RE GETTING IT ALL WRONG IN CHURCH PLANTING

To me church planting or church planters fall into one of two categories ... and there's not really that much common ground in between. I would also contend that this reflects our understanding of the gospel and the mission of God. You either have a church planter launching a worship service from scratch or you have a church planter engaging in missionary activity that will ultimately see a new community form around people responding to the gospel. See the difference? It's subtle. It's also significant and profound.

We've also seen this distinction play out during this global COVID-19 pandemic. Many church planters are scrambling to try and replicate a Sunday worship experience but somehow do it online. Whereas others are scrambling to mobilize and release their people to love and serve their communities. Obviously, it's not either/or but both/and. I'm not harboring any conspiracy theories nor trying to pick fights. What I have observed over the last nearly two decades in church planting is that there's a difference ... and it's a big one.

I distinguish the two by calling one a "church planting pastor" and the other a "church planting missionary." Ten minutes into a conversation with a church planter I can tell which one they are. The church planting pastor talks about the worship services, the influential pastors and preachers in their lives, what kind of music they will use on Sundays, the cool venue where they hope to meet, what and for how long they will preach, the Bible commentaries they're reading, and so on.

What do I hear from the church planting missionary? Well, that's another story. Conversations about the people. People in their neighborhood, town, or city they're trying to connect with, love, and serve. I hear and see their broken hearts.

There's a deep yearning and longing for people to identify as followers of Jesus. I also hear brokenness over injustices in their neighborhoods and cities.

To me, these conversations are the number one indicator of whether a church planter will stay long-term or jump ship once the numbers in their worship services don't grow like they hoped. You see, one longs for, aches for, and breaks for people in the neighborhood, town, or city. The other? They long for a growing throng of people on Sundays so they can dedicate more time to sermon prep, growing their platform, and the like. Don't believe me? It's all over their church's Instagram feed.

In the end, there's nothing wrong with either approach (minus the innate narcissism of the former). Seriously. I don't cry foul. Nor would I belittle or berate. Maybe it was simply because I was never very good at pulling off the on-stage dude wooing people into a gathering to hear my teachings. Maybe I just never was cool enough to pull that off. Don't get me wrong ... we need teaching, times of celebrating together, and the like. However, if you're wired for mission you find your mind and imagination drifting towards how to connect with people who have zero interest in trendy gatherings for trendy Christians. To that end, and in alignment with the metanarrative of the mission of God, that's why we start things ... businesses, non-profits ... and engage in activities like advocacy, addressing injustices, because our heart bleeds and yearns for this planet and the people made in God's image who dwell on it.

I titled this chapter "We're Getting It All Wrong In Church Planting" for a reason. So how or where have we gotten it wrong? By removing church planting from the larger scope of the mission of God and what he wills to accomplish in and through us. We know that it goes far beyond simply populating heaven. It's about redeeming life in the here and now. That includes people, but it also embraces the economies of our communities, environmental issues, and so much more.

Church planting is an exciting adventure and endeavor. And it gets more exciting when we move the locus of our activities and endeavors away from Sundays without doing away with them.

CH 15

WHAT CHURCH PLANTING
SHOULD LOOK LIKE

Recently I took a road trip with two of my sons to central Oregon. We now have a routine when traveling and exploring. We drive to where we're going, park, get out on foot and explore, take photos, drink coffee, and talk. Our last trip was no different. The only thing that changes is geography. Sometimes all we do is explore Portland neighborhoods. But this last trip was rural Oregon.

The first town we came to was Dufur. We found a place to park (which wasn't difficult at all) and set out on foot. Their "downtown" comprised only a block or two. But there was plenty to see. We talked about architecture, rural culture and sensibilities, and of course ... their economy. What type of industry is there? How do people earn a living? Why does everyone drive a big pickup truck? How much or little are they influenced by Portland less than an hour and a half away?

After a bit we piled back into our SUV and kept driving. Next stop? Maupin. Since economics was already on our minds and radar, we noticed something different as we approached Maupin. From newer and nicer homes to the ubiquitous presence of whitewater rafting companies it truly had a different vibe. While Maupin felt bigger than Dufur the reality is it isn't (Maupin has a population of 437; Dufur has 638). The key was and is economics. You see, economics is not simply about money (which it certainly is!!!) but it's also about our wellbeing and that of our communities. In other words, in the same way that our life rises and falls based upon income so does that of a community. Probably even more. Also tied into this is a sense of identity.

Sure, you may scoff at this as being shallow and misguided, but hear me out. Let's look at larger cities. What's the biggest different between the Bay Area and Detroit? It's their economies. Detroit has been struggling hard for decades. They went from 1.8 million people in 1950 to 700,000 today. Why? Economic decline … more like a freefall. Detroit has a poverty rate nearly three times higher than the national average—roughly 35 percent. San Francisco, the center of the tech universe, is humming along quite well. It wasn't too long ago that Detroit held that position as the center of the universe for the automobile industry.

Financial health has a massive impact upon our wellbeing and identity. There's an enormous difference between owning your own home and saving for retirement compared to eking out a living … in Section 8 housing, with kids on free lunches at school, and grocery shopping with food stamps. Economics matter. A lot.

Whether we're talking about urban or rural communities one of the key indicators of health and wellbeing is tied into economics. So, church planer … missionary … pastor, would it be a stretch to reason that your role goes far beyond gathering people on Sundays, helping them to pray and read their Bible more, and getting them to volunteer in the nursery? If so, then what's beyond that? I turn to Christopher Wright who brings us back to the mission of God … the mission we find ourselves on. He writes:

What is the mission of God's people?

- We are here as human being to care for God's creation.
- We are chosen in Abraham to be a people through whom God's blessing reaches all nations.
- We are called to walk in the ways of God, in justice and righteousness, in a corrupt world.
- We are to live out the dynamic of our own redemption in our compassionate treatment of others.[1]

Wright's list is longer but I'll stop there. Do you see it? Again, this does not dismiss the importance of gathering for worship and instruction on Sundays as well as those other activities that foster spiritual formation. But my point is we are not merely spiritual beings as followers of Jesus. We're also tied to our location which includes its economics. To put it another way, the last thing I'm interested in is what your cool gathering looks like. Nor do I care how many followers you have on Instagram … but

---

[1] Wright, *The Mission of God's People*, 164.

that photo with the purchased Lightroom preset of you teaching, tattooed arm outstretched, does look pretty dope.

What if we focused as much time and energy seeking the betterment of our neighborhoods, towns, and cities? If we led with that .... instead of the typical "What will my worship service look like?" ... what inevitably will happen is we will find ourselves immersed in the stream of the mission of God. The mission of God encompasses everything ... the physical, the economic, the spiritual worlds. Wouldn't it therefore make sense for that to be a key facet of church planting?

What that looks like is this ... there is NO separation between what we do on Sundays and with launching businesses and non-profits, engaging in community and economic development, and addressing the other justice issues around us the rest of the week. It is in the combination of these disparate pieces that we create the beautiful mosaic that is church planting. No preset or filter could make it look any better.

I get it. I know we're held to the standard definition of success based on how many people we can gather in one place on a Sunday. Our funding is tied to it. Unfortunately, so are our identities. But what if we saw church planting as a holistic adventure that encompassed more than your ability to gather a lot of people in one room for an hour and fifteen minutes one day a week? What if we saw our role as tying our very lives to the health and wellbeing of our neighborhoods, towns, and cities as we help them flourish with new businesses, non-profits, advocacy work, and more?

Watch out, if you try it you might realize how much you've been missing ... and you will be hooked.

CH 16

SPOILER ALERT: MOST CHURCH PLANTERS ARE NOT VERY ENTREPRENEURIAL

The longer I work alongside and interact with church planters the clearer the divide becomes between those who're entrepreneurial and those who think they are. While it is assumed that all church planters are entrepreneurial by nature because they're starting a church seemingly from scratch … that simply isn't true.

There are a lot of church planters out there who really are pastors, teachers, or managers looking to start a church. In other words, their main focus on starting a new church is so they can teach, counsel, shepherd, manage, and perform other pastoral duties. I call them *church planting pastors.*

They aren't really that entrepreneurial. It takes all of their effort and energy simply to focus on starting a new church (... or worship service). Any thought of being bivocational or starting a business or non-profit on top of planting seems absurd to them. I hear it regularly: "I can't imagine launching a startup AND planting a church at the same time." That simply means they've tapped into what little entrepreneurial spirit they have to try and start a church. If they are forced to go the bivocational route it means they will ultimately latch onto some other job rather than look at starting something else. Church planting pastors also represent the largest portion of church planters today.

On the other hand, church planting missionaries are a different breed. We may call them serial entrepreneurs. They start things because they can't help it. To them it seems absurd NOT to start other initiatives while they plant a church. On top of that, because our coaching relationships are full of these types, I hear just as much zeal, passion, and excitement about both what they're starting and the church they are planting. Sometimes maybe even a little more. Why? Because what they're starting allows them to intersect with those who have no interest in church. This energizes church planting missionaries.

While it is easy to point out and identify some of these differences it's another to watch how this plays out in day-to-day life for church planters. Why? Because usually those who're funding them, overseeing them, coaching them, etc., tend to be more risk-adverse and managerial. They might secretly love spreadsheets and flowcharts. As a result, they work best with planters who're more church planting pastors because they "get them." Church planting missionaries are misfits in the truest sense because they march to the beat of a different drummer. They end up "getting in trouble" with those in their denominations overseeing them because they simply think and act differently.

Let me be clear. I'm not trying to pit one group against another. Nor am I saying that there's anything wrong nor dubious with any of these categories. It is simply for us to take stock, self-assess, and learn more how we're wired and gifted.

So what is the point in all of this? You need to discover who you are ... and once you begin to find out to stick with it. You can only be you. That's why uniform training for church planters doesn't work. They tend to favor only one group (church planting pastors) and not appeal to the other. Also, often times strings are attached to funding that pressure church planters to fit the mold designed for them. But my hunch is even though they did their required training to qualify for funding they were squirming and bored throughout the process.

One of the activities and assessments we do in our cohorts is to find out what kind of entrepreneur you are. Even among those who are entrepreneurial there are still many variations. Some are disruptors, others take risks, others are great at selling and wooing, and so on. The key is to understand who you are to not only plant, but also to launch your startup with your skills and traits in mind. There's only one you. No need to wear the masks of others. Be you.

CH 17

THE MYTHOLOGY OF CALLING

What exactly is a calling? What does it look like on a practical and everyday level? Is it a feeling? A hunch? Intuition? A burning bush moment where God meets us face-to-face? These are easy questions to ask. What is difficult is precisely how to answer them. We hear and see all kinds of ways people describe calling. In the end we're left scratching our collective heads in confusion.

How do we really know?

Beyond that, other questions surface. Who exactly is called? Is it only those who get paid to do ministry? Pastors ... church planters ... missionaries.

Is that it? Are they the only ones whom God calls and everyone else is left to figure things out on their own? Does calling warrant or necessitate an ability to derive one's income from what they're called to? Should that be the deciding factor?

You see, there's a lot of mythology related to calling. It's almost to the point where we need to slide it in the lineup next to Bigfoot, the Loch Ness monster, and UFOs. Makes sense to me. Why is calling so shrouded in legend, lore, and mystery? It also doesn't help that most often how people use the term cannot really be traced throughout the story arc of Scripture. Some contend it's more about understanding how God has wired us whereas other speak in terms of supernatural and spectacular revelation (e.g., Moses and the burning bush).

These questions are actually central to the terrain that Intrepid treads upon. Ultimately, when planters are looking to plant a church … and in particular launch a startup as part of their strategy what they're really wrestling with is calling. Am I called to do this? I thought my calling was exclusively to plant a church. Does launching a social enterprise take away from my calling?

This conversation is nuanced. It doesn't help that there are many who love to toss around this saying ... "God's will done God's way will not lack God's resources." That is code for "You're doing something wrong if you're not paid full-time to do this." That causes a lot of shame and guilt in many ministry leaders.

We need to demythologize calling. No, not de-spiritualize it. But take it out of legend and lore and bring it back into practical and everyday life. Precisely where it needs to be.

While time and space does not permit me to really explore the nuances of calling, what I'd like to do here briefly is ask questions. Think of me as a medical doctor and you as my patient with some kind of ailment. Through the course of our initial meeting (after I wash my hands) I ask you a battery of questions. What I'm trying to do is diagnose what is ailing you so I can create some sort of treatment plan going forward. The same would be helpful in terms of calling.

What are you processing? Are you leaning into one direction or another? How did you arrive at this place? Based on your theological leanings and spiritual upbringing, how do you view calling? Are only paid ministry professionals called? What if you're also an accountant, a librarian, an attorney, a nurse, a pro athlete ... are you still called? Does calling necessitate that you step away from your career to move full-time into paid ministry? If you're planting a church ... why can't you launch a social enterprise while you plant? If Paul could have a successful and lasting ministry while only doing it part-time, what's stopping you?

While I may not know enough to prescribe a treatment plan we can at least begin answering these questions. More important is saying things out loud. Whether we're talking to a counselor or a medical doctor, there's something freeing about verbalizing what we're struggling with. That's a big step forward. My hunch is we have a lot of maladies in our understanding of calling. As we process them and say them out loud we'll probably realize that much of it (not all) is an aberration that really isn't normative in Scripture.

What this means ... and I'm going out on a limb here with my preliminary diagnosis ... is you're probably a lot more free to pursue creative ministry than you might realize. It may be that launching a startup while you're planting a church or whatever is burdening you or piquing your heart and interests. Obviously, seeking sound wisdom is important, but be forewarned that this also can be the same as trying to self-diagnose through WebMD or asking a friend what's wrong with you. We're not the only ones wrestling with calling. We're all in the same boat and filtering this conversation through our own worldview and theological camp. (Don't worry, we all do. I just did.)

My goal is to see you're not boxed in. Did Paul really have to push himself to make tents while he did missionary work? He probably didn't even think about it. We find nothing in his letters where he struggled with it other than stating that while he certainly has the right to expect his ministry gig to be paid and full-time he opted instead to work with his hands so as to not be a burden to the church. That makes me like Paul even more.

CH 18

RETHINKING CHURCH PLANTING FUNDING ... NO JOB, NO FUNDING

I am fortunate to be a friend and confidant to many church planters. I am regularly in text communication, having conversations via social media, or meeting face-to-face. I cherish these conversations. More importantly, I value these relationships.

Maybe it's because I lead Intrepid where my focus is helping church planters, missionaries, and pastors launch startups that I'm often talking about funding with these leaders. I've heard every funding story under the sun. From the million-dollar church planter raking in six figures a year to the church planter who sunk his life savings into simply moving to another place. Most planters fall somewhere in between. Regardless, the conversation most often revolves around funding.

Usually the funding question is framed in a question, "How can I stay here long-term?" Those who come with nothing are nimble from the get-go (they have to be) and pivot immediately into bivocational work. Those who have the dream scenario of abundant funding simply have a longer leash until they too are doing the same. Most often these well-compensated planters end up blowing through all of their funding before they too are scrambling for part- or full-time work. Having watched this storyline play out time and time again, if I were a denominational or church planting organization leader here's what I'd do going forward ...

If you don't get a job while you plant you won't receive any funding from us. Period.

Church planting is an investment. Honestly it's one of the worst investments any supporter, donor, or church can make. It's like trying to buy stock in

Blockbuster video or Blackberry phones. The ROI is horrible. It's not worth it. At all.

Think along with me … Why do we think it is a good investment for church planters to receive $300,000 to $1 million just so they can grab Christians from other churches? That's how 99 percent of church planting works. How horrible an investment is that? "You mean it costs that much just to move sheep from one pen to another?"

To be clear, I'm not saying funding is wrong or bad. I would simply expect a church planter to get some kind of job. Why? Roots. Long-term commitment. Often times once church planters blow through their money they simply up and move on to their next ministry venture. They're like an Instagram influencer jet-setting to their next paid gig. Sure, in their newsletter they'll share how "dark" their city is and how people are "unresponsive to the gospel" as they seamlessly slip into their new ministry role. But if from the beginning you have a job, that tells me you're playing the long game. You're there to see it through.

Most church planters think they're going to "hit it" and be the next big deal. So they wait, holding out hope, even praying and fasting towards that end, only to realize their dream of planting a church that pays them a full-time salary is evaporating right before their eyes. What is my advice to them?

Get a job.

Or, if you have a longer runway because of the support you've raised, take time to launch a business or non-profit. There are no guarantees, but between your support and a job you're at least moving in the direction of long-term financial sustainability.

Listen, while I'm a big fan of church planting AND church planters, I believe our system is broken. Severely. We can either throw more money into it … more assessments, upgraded training, etc., or we can pivot before it's too late.

CH 19

THERE'S ONE THING THAT WILL KEEP YOU IN PLACE LONG TERM AND IT'S NOT A MYSTERY

The only time I ever left a church planting venture was because of money ... or the lack thereof. Therefore, I don't write this from the vantage point of being afar, aloof, or arrived. I failed. Miserably. I know that if finances or funding were not an issue I'd still be church planting in my previous stops.

Looking back over the past several months of articles I've written I readily admit that I've taken the gloves off ... bypassed any filters I might've put in place and simply tried to state the obvious ... and holding back no punches. Again, it's not because I've arrived or I'm standing on a pinnacle of great success trying to woo church planting travelers my way. Instead, I'm sitting on the side of the road in a broken down car with smoke billowing from an overheated engine. Cracked block.

Last week, I had two remarkable conversations about church planting, missions, and funding. One was with a board member of a missions organization. The other was with a senior director of a missions organization overseeing ministry in a massive swath of the Asian continent. During the course of these conversations we talked lots about international missions, social entrepreneurship, and the funding dilemma that every North American church planter faces.

It's not that it is any different outside of one's home country, it's simply there's a better framework for funding. Imagine sending a church planting couple anywhere outside the borders of their home country ... and to play with themes addressed in Intrepid ... this couple is moving into Dharavi (one of Asia's largest slum communities located in Mumbai). How odd would it be for a funding strategy if they only received three-to-five years of support with the hope that by the time their funding ran dry they'll have gathered enough people to sustain them financially. Yeah ... that sounds weird, doesn't it?

But what if they launched an NGO focused on architecture and urban planning? And what if their work was primarily to work with the people to come up with better design solutions for more permanent housing? Not only would they be a blessing and an asset to the people of Dharavi, but their focus would be on empowerment rather that "doing" ministry. Also, because of their NGO status, they've been able to secure grants and outside funding ... even from the government ... for their work. As a result, they have funding to sustain them long-term.

My whole premise behind Intrepid is simply this ... what if we did those kinds of things *here* that we routinely do over *there*? That's it. Nothing new. It's not rocket science. It's hardly noteworthy. It is simply doing what we send missionaries to do outside our international borders.

So why can't we do that here? Not only would church planters be more active in seeking the betterment of their communities, but they would be securing funding that is not tied to their "performance" as church planters. That would mean more planters could freely move into lower-income communities with no hesitation or strings attached.

Instead of asking "why?" what if instead we asked "why not?" Why not take this approach in church planting? Is it because you "want to be the man?" Because you "have to" preach? Because it doesn't line up with your personal brand and social media platform? Why not do more church planting like this?

CH 20

WHAT YOU'RE MISSING
ABOUT BIVOCATIONAL
CHURCH PLANTING

Even though bivocational ministry or church planting has now become mainstream it certainly hasn't become mainstream in the hearts of church planters. There's also a disconnect. I hear repeatedly from church planters who share their frustrations with me with the fact that the guys in their denominations or networks who're telling them to be bivo all seem to have comfortable full-time ministry gigs. Many entities, orgs, denominations, and ministries (like Intrepid) are beating the drum of bivo church planting, but let's have some honest conversations.

Yes, all things #bivo are hot right now. It's the trend, the fad, the thing to do. But like I said, I also believe that we love the IDEA of bivo more than we love actually being bivo. For most, what I am really hearing is that bivocational church planting truly is a last resort after they run out of funding. So how and why are we championing something that most church planters would rather not do? It reminds me of an undergrad course I teach.

Every fall I teach a university course for incoming freshman called Bicycles, Equity, and Race: Urban Mobility in Portland. The premise is we use the bike to explore the intersection of affordable transportation, gentrification, race, and equity in the city. When I say "use the bike" I don't mean we literally bike all over Portland. Why? Most students are terrified to bike. Sure, we'll do a fun bike ride on touristy quad-bikes along the downtown waterfront, but that's about it.

In "America's Bicycle Capital," students who grew up here are not willing to bike. "It's too dangerous," they tell me. So they drive. Regardless of what I think about bicycles and the fact I bike all over the city every week, it's another thing to try and convince students to do the same. Until it gets safer and more accessible like in Denmark they simply won't do it.

Why would I beat the drum they MUST bike if they don't deem it safe? With all of the transportation options available, why would I insist they use the one that scares them the most? I see bivo church planting the same way in terms of convincing church planters to do the same.

With that said, I have been able to identify what the hang-up (at least one of) is for church planters. It is this ... bivo church planting means for many of them working some job outside of ministry that you're not particularly skilled at nor passionate about. In other words, it's a drain. I agree. If you're not doing something you're skilled at nor passionate about it really is a drain. The solution? You need to do something you're skilled at and passionate about.

If you've followed my writings you know I say a good bit about my experiences as a hiking and mountain biking guide while I planted my first church in Tucson. I did it over a five-year stretch. While there was a lot that I truly loved about it, the truth is that after a while I was over it. Ready to move on. It definitely was good for a season and I learned lots. But to make a career out of it? I wasn't interested. The parts of the job I did enjoy were more about studying the urban archaeology and human history of the area, in particular all the Hohokam pit houses and pottery we found. It was during this time that I decided to pursue a doctorate in urban studies.

Now compare that to me teaching a full course load every semester. I can't get enough of it. I love what I do. I get geeked out when I'm asked to teach a new course because it means copious amounts of reading and prep. Sometimes I love the prep more than the teaching. Also, for me, there's nothing better than to be in the classroom and on campus. I love university students. I love teaching and facilitating discussions, taking them throughout the city to learn and explore, and seeing their "a-ha" moments. Half my life is doing that; the other half is leading Intrepid.

See the difference? When most think of bivo church planting their thoughts go to having to do something they can't stomach just to get you by in hopes that their new church actually takes off so they can devote their full time to it. That is a night and day difference from doing something "outside" of church planting that you're equally passionate about. I can honestly say this … when I wake up my mind immediately turns to reading and prepping for my classes … and I'm giddy. That's a far cry from waking up at 4:30am to get to the shop early to lead hikes on a trail I had literally been on over 600 times. Don't get me wrong … work is work. There's always a mundaneness about it, but it either lights your fires or dampens them.

Do I think everyone HAS to be bivo? No, not at all. Some of you have connections to deep pockets and come from parts of the country that have a lot of churches who're willing to support you. If that's you, then go for it. Just talk to me when you run out of money, though, and then we can explore bivo more. (Wink.)

What might you be missing about bivocational church planting? No one is telling you that you have to work at some lousy job that you hate. Admittedly, we certainly can talk this way if we're from a place of privilege in the U.S. and Canada. We know these realities are not uniform across the globe. So let me ask you a question. Apart from reading books, tweeting, and prepping sermons, what are you passionate about? What industry? What career? Business? Law? Medicine? Education? Food and beverage?

The goal for bivo church planting isn't to shoehorn you into a career you hate. You wouldn't last anyway if that were true. You'd jump at the chance of a pastoral role at your buddy's church. But in reality, it's more about knowing who you are, what you're good at, and what you're passionate about. Also ... and I've written much about this elsewhere (see my book *The Adventure of Vocation*) ... this means you digging deeper into your calling. Who are you? How did God wire you? What shaping experiences have you had? What can you do? What do you want to do? What should you do? You need to wrestle with these questions. It's okay.

There are a lot of voices out there shaping and influencing this whole bivo church planting conversation. There are also a lot of niceties coming from non-practitioners and theorists. You need to own this conversation. Wade through the noise and do some deep work of the soul. My hunch is there's a lot more that you can offer the world that would go hand-in-hand with the church you're trying to plant. Maybe you simply need to give yourself permission to dream and explore. If you want to talk and process this I'd be glad to be your sounding board. I'm here for you.

CH 21

BUT I DON'T WANT TO BE BIVOCATIONAL ...

I rarely come across a church planter who voluntarily ventures into bivocational church planting. Sure, there are many who are bivo. But out of necessity. It's also unfortunately reflective of what I'd call the deep-rooted injustices in our ministry world. What I mean is that more often than not "ethnic" church planters are bivocational from the very beginning. Because the funds they receive from a denomination or network are negligible at best. But most white planters? Well, that's a different story.

There, I said it out loud. But we all know this. It shouldn't be this way.

Who wants to be intentionally bivocational from the get-go if they don't have to? I rarely, and I mean rarely find a planter choosing this route. We talked about this last week in one of our coaching calls. For many, this idea of being bivocational is a distraction and pulls you away from actual church planting. PLUS, if you as a planter have any ministry degrees and even advanced degrees this makes it even more challenging. "Come on, I have a Master's degree. I shouldn't have to work some crap job I don't want to. It's my right as one who is educated to do this (church planting) full time."

There's probably a very small percentage of church planters who not only decide to be bivocational from the start, but who also intentionally plan to start a business or non-profit as part of the planting process. When I first ventured into church planting, did I even have it on my radar to start a business or non-profit as part of my church planting strategy? No, not even close. I didn't even know that option existed. While I was ultimately "forced" to become bivocational simply as a means of survival it certainly wasn't my preferred future. I didn't anticipate it. I wasn't overly thrilled about it.

And yet, it became the very thing that changed me and altered the trajectory of my life and ministry.

Church planting is difficult. Incredibly stressful. It is not for the faint of heart. Despite the high probability of failure many take the plunge. Since planters are putting all of their eggs into one planting basket then it makes sense why they want to be all-in on planting full-time rather than be "distracted" by working some other job. Again, especially if you hold any advanced degrees related to ministry (e.g., MDiv). What if that's you and you don't want to be bivocational?

Don't.

Seriously, you don't have it. To repeat ... church planters in North America are often times free to choose whether they want to be bivocational or not. This isn't true across the board. It's also not true globally. And yet the great irony is it seems as though the churches with the greatest fruit and staying power are usually planted by an "ethnic" church planter. (Note, I use the term "ethnic" since it is often used to denote all non-white church planters which again only reinforces things like white privilege, etc. Don't believe me? I've seen it first-hand repeatedly in denominational work.)

I'll say this ... if you don't want to be bivocational then don't. You don't have to. No one is forcing you to. Sure, after year five and your plant isn't "blowing up" we can talk, but until then? You do you. Those who're coming around Intrepid are making the decision from the outset to not only be bivocational but make starting a business or non-profit their church planting strategy. It's all intrinsically linked. It's one. Just like you would put on soccer camps and use mission teams from small-town Texas or suburban Georgia to staff them, these planters are utilizing their startups as their church planting strategy. The only difference is this is building a legitimate missionary platform (let's be honest, most of those soccer camps aren't that well-run or effective) and working to ensure you're putting down roots and long-term sustainability.

You do you, but I'm throwing my lot in with the bivo peeps and the "ethnic" planters.

CH 22

SHOULD EVERY CHURCH PLANTER START A SIDE HUSTLE?

I get asked this question a lot … should every church planter start a side hustle? Interestingly, it usually comes from well-funded church planters who have no interest in starting a business or non-profit. Why would they? They're not scraping by or needing to create additional income streams. But what about the other 99 percent of church planters? Should they? Should you?

It depends.

Yesterday I was rereading *The Celtic Way of Evangelism* by George Hunter. I'm teaching a course this semester at Multnomah University called Global Evangelism and Discipleship and Hunter's book is one of the required texts. It's a phenomenal book. It is so applicable to the landscape of church planting today that it is almost prophetic. I came across this quote that stopped me in my tracks ... "No major denomination in the United States regards apostolic ministry to card-carrying, secular, pre-Christians outsiders as its priority or even as normal ministry."[1]

Wait, what? Is that even true? It didn't take me long to answer with a resounding "YES!" It is true. Now mind you, what we say will obviously be different. I also know without a doubt that our intentions and motives are true and noble. We want to see people become citizens of the Kingdom and live under the new reality of a gracious and loving King. However, that's where it ends. Because what Hunter describes is what we do and even our metrics for funding church planting go against our best intentions and motives. How so?

You've heard me say repeatedly that our current funding models mean one thing and one thing alone in church planting ... they are designed for and predicated on transfer growth. In other words,

---

[1] Hunter, *The Celtic Way of Evangelism*, 13.

due to the nature of the timeline of church planting, if any church planter has a shot at actually "making it" that means he must woo Christians from other churches. At best they snag lapsed Christians back into the faith community.

If actually reaching those who claim no church affiliation nor interest in God is your aim, then given our current church planting funding models, you're doomed to failure before you even start. Because to do that will take years ... even decades to see any traction. If that is truly your desire then what you need to do is figure out how to be financially sustainable long-term. For some, that will mean launching a side hustle (I actually abhor that term, but that's for another conversation). For others it means stepping into a career outside of ministry. If that is true, then what do you want to do? What is your preferred future towards long-term financial self-sustainability in ministry? Startup? Jump into a new job or career?

If I were you I'd begin the church planting journey with that in mind rather than wait until years five or seven and have that "ah crap!" moment where you're left scrambling to piece things together. That's if you actually want to. Many will simply jet set to their next ministry assignment once they've blown through all of the funds they raised.

Should every church planter launch a startup then? For some it could be the very vehicle for long-term rootedness. For others, what career could you step into that will achieve the same outcome?

CH 23

CAN YOU REALLY START A CHURCH AND LAUNCH A STARTUP WITH ZERO MONEY?

Shortly after we moved to Portland ten years ago I began attending Portland State University. Early on I connected with one of the professors who taught in the urban studies program. His name is Charles Heying (a fellow Iowa native). He had written a book called *Brew to Bikes: Portland's Artisan Economy*. It explores the unique nature of Portland's artisan or maker economy. Since that day I've used the book repeatedly in classes as well as in our Intrepid coaching.

Heying does a masterful job of laying out the economic transition to a Post-Fordist economy. As he explores the rise of the creative economy we can see how it plays out in multiple ways ... tech, the arts, and yes, in making many other things... coffee, beer, clothes, wine, and more. He calls it the "artisan economy."

One quote in the book, to put it bluntly and plainly, changed my life. As Heying was listing the organization of artisan work, he highlights what he calls the "art of assemblage:"

> The ability to assemble human, financial, and physical capital is remarkably fluid in the artisan economy. The audacious artisan can literally start from nothing and, with pluck and luck, build a substantial organization that can survive at any niche or level personally suited to the artisan entrepreneur.[1]

The first time I read that literally my first reaction was ... why don't we think that way in church planting?

Wait, you mean start with NOTHING? No hundreds of thousands of raised dollars, no overhead, or anything else? Yes, yes indeed. Now

---

[1] Heying, *Brew to Bikes*, 47.

mind you, not all artisan startups are the same. They vary in the amount of equipment needed to begin. But as I read Heying's book I detected almost a biblical sense of calling and vocation for these artisans. Nothing would deter them from starting ... not even if they had little to no funds.

My next thought was ... why not? Why not me? Since then I've started three companies from scratch. No money. No overhead. It was an experiment. I wanted to see if I actually could do it, scale up, and more. While I don't claim to be a business guru by any stretch ... plus there's a big difference between starting and scaling up ... the point is that it can be done. As Heying notes, it takes audacity and pluck.

There are a lot of supposed "shoulds" in both the church planting and startup worlds. Church planters "should" have hundreds of thousands of dollars committed before moving to their new city to plant. Startup entrepreneurs "should" have hundreds of thousands of dollars ... millions in money raised. But having money doesn't guarantee anything. If anything, it simply delays the inevitable ... failure. It means more resources are squandered. And it certainly doesn't guarantee success. But do you know what is nearly guaranteed success? Being sustainable ... financially self-sufficient from DAY ONE. (Again, I need to reiterate I am speaking in generalities as not all business startups are the same.)

You see, the problem isn't funding, but our models. We've also seen this in our current COVID-19 crisis that is affecting millions and millions of Americans. Churches or startups with a model dependent on a lot of overhead and such, that weren't sustainable since the vey beginning, are feeling the effects. If that is you, I know it is terrifying and brutally painful. This is not about me wagging my finger at you. I'm talking about going forward.

The issue is neither church planting nor startups, but our models of funding. I'm now more convinced than ever that if a church planter isn't starting some kind of business or non-profit (or working bivocationally) they shouldn't receive any funding. How many millions of dollars are thrown away each year because we have an ineffective and inefficient model? All so Church Planter A can move to City B and then proceed to gather Christians from area churches? Yes, that was my own experience as a church planter. Guilty as charged. But that is precisely what the vast percentage of church planting in North America looks like.

We need a new funding model. One of the keys to creating that model is found in artisan entrepreneurs. As Heying notes, "The audacious artisan can literally start from nothing."[2] May we go and do likewise.

---

[2] Ibid.

AWKWRD

WHY SOLO CHURCH PLANTING IS CAREER SUICIDE

Yes, I said it … "career suicide." If you want to ruin your reputation, crater your credit score, and have little to nothing to show for your efforts … move across the country with a vision, a prayer, and your family, land in a new city, and attempt to plant a church from scratch. Who'd sign up for THAT?

Most church planters I know do. (I did … twice.)

Am I being a bit melodramatic? Probably, but not as much as you'd think. I've seen the same storyline in every city I've lived in … Tucson, Vancouver (BC), and now Portland. Once in a while there's an anomaly, an exception, an outlier, a church plant that "sticks," but for the most part that's the cold hard reality. Denominations won't tell you that. Church planting networks don't divulge this reality. The only way to find out is after you've fallen flat on your face. When you're on the ground, at your lowest, you look up and go, "What the h$#% just happened?"

Now, are you ready for the good news?

It doesn't have to be that way. It really comes down to this … you have two options for church planting. As I lay these out, know that I'm speaking in generalities because there are anomalies all over the map. Ready? Here we go:

Option 1 - Imbed yourself in a church planting church and plant out from there.

Option 2 - Self-identify as a missionary and live like one.

Yes, there are more options but two is all I have the attention span for today. The point is, most church plants, unless you're hiving off from a larger church will inevitably struggle and eke out an unspectacular existence. Sooner or later the planter / pastor tires of leading a congregation of thirty or fifty or seventy-five people. Often times there's the realization that in order to keep going the planter needs to move into the bivocational world. Since that is not the desired path of most planters then usually after six-to-ten years it's time to move on.

Conversely, if I ever were to "plant a church" (conventionally-speaking) then I'd be foolish not to imbed in and plant out of a larger church planting church. There's an enormous difference launching with 200 people compared to twenty (including two denomination reps, your parents, and your church planting buddy in the city and his family). So what is the solution?

Become a missionary.

The truth is, and you already know this, there are multiple avenues to take in church planting. The best "guarantee" in planting is to hive off from the mothership. If not, then live like a missionary. Take it slow, and reap a harvest for the long term. As I said, there are always church plants that "pop." But the truth that we don't want to hear is that more than likely that will not be you ... or me. It definitely was not me. I'm no alpha and not a big woo guy. I'm not a social glue guy. I'd rather sit in a coffee shop reading academic journals on the creative economy and how that reshapes life in cities.

My job is to help you simply think things through and to do so before you sell the farm, burn the bridge, mess up your credit, shake your family foundation, and then ultimately crumble as your denomination and funders start tightening the vice grip on you and your funding because you haven't "popped" yet. I want to save you from this anguish.

Spoiler alert: you can actually plant in a way that is healthy and life-giving. But that takes time. To self-identify as a missionary and plant from the harvest will take AT LEAST ten years before there's any noticeable fruit or movement. But I'm guessing you knew that going in which is why you intentionally stepped into bivocational church planting (if you chose that route).

You got this. Hang in there.

CH 25

HOW DO YOU KNOW WHEN TO GIVE UP ON YOUR CHURCH PLANT?

I gave up on the first church I ever planted. I walked away. The follow-up questions then went something like this ... Why would I give up on something I poured my blood, sweat, and tears into? What would compel me to leave something for which I sacrificed everything?

Many church planters I know are in the same dilemma. Now most probably would never admit it. Oh, but they know deep in their hearts it's not panning out how they hoped and dreamed. Three to five years ago as they were rumbling down the interstate driving their rented twenty-five-foot moving truck to their new city all they could think of were the possibilities. A new church, built from scratch, attracting throngs of people. Rapid growth. Momentum. All of the things we dream about when we plant a church.

We can imagine ourselves standing on stage with an expensive headset mic on. Perfect hair and a well-manicured beard. With a Bible in one hand and the other hand resting on the podium with the new iPad that we use for sermon notes. We woo the crowd with our biblical insights conveyed with wit and charm. Fast forward three or four years. No expensive headset mic. No crowds. Just a handful of people who could probably all fit in your living room. Your iPad is old, clunky, and slow.

Is it time to give up?

How do you know when to walk away? How do you know when to burrow in deeper and keep on plowing?

Every church planter faces these questions. At times numbers don't even matter. I know pastors who'd love nothing more than to quietly slip away from the church they helped launch, even if it was one of the few that actually took off. How do you know it's time to throw in the towel?

This is complicated. Very complicated. There are simply too many variables at hand. One trend that I have observed is that locals who plant have a much higher stick-rate than the outsiders. Think about it. If you're already home, there's no "going home" if it doesn't work out. For everyone else, you're not home. When you mention the word "home" or think about where home, then where you're living now is not your home. Therefore, when the bottom drops out it is easy to long for home. But if you're already home when that happens? You have no place else to go.

But that still doesn't answer the question ... How do you know when to give up on your church plant? For me, it all goes back to calling. Yes, calling. It's a word that we covet and at times wield like a Jedi light saber to ward off those who doubt us. But seriously, that's why I make blanket statements like, "Most church planters I meet are not really called." For many, it's a good idea, a career change, or a way to strike out on their own. But a calling?

I'm also not saying if you do walk away it wasn't necessarily because you weren't called in the first place. However, it is something to think about. If you were convinced enough to leave everything in order to plant then why would you want to bail after a few years because the numbers aren't there? A deep sense of calling helps you navigate those dark nights of the soul. Now back to my story.

Why did I walk away from my new church plant? Simple. Calling. Or, at least what I perceived as calling. You see, when I moved to the city where I first planted, my dream was about a multiplication of churches. A year after we began meeting publicly my denomination asked me to instead become the regional church planting strategist. My task? To plant as many churches as we could (i.e., multiplication) ... but not by me. In order to do so I had to hand off my church plant to someone else. Since my dream was for multiplication it was a no-brainer. Over the next three years we started twelve churches. It was one of the best decisions of my life.

It was about my calling. The elders of my church plant affirmed that this was a better fit for me. I like books over people and am kind of an ideas person. I'm not a "woo" type of guy and I'm not very gregarious. So becoming a strategist was my wheelhouse.

I must've forgotten that lesson because after moving to the Pacific Northwest I tried and failed two more times to plant. The first time we got our funding yanked after eighteen months because we weren't progressing as fast as our denomination wanted. The second time? A year or so into it I lost my stomach for it, especially for the machinery of church planting and all that goes into it. I walked away before we ever met publicly. In both cases I have no regrets. Why?

Because of calling. In the 1990s we felt God place within us a burden for the Pacific Northwest. That was long before I even knew anything about church planting. I hadn't been on staff at a church or done anything in formal ministry. I was just a college dude who had a crazy ministry experience and encounter with God that redirected my life. As a result, I felt called to the PNW and it wasn't tied to church planting in the sense of me having to be a planter. However, today? My life revolves around church planting.

So there you have it ... three stories of my own failed attempts at planting where I did NOT stick it out. (I'll let you in on a little secret. Whenever I write most often I'm really speaking to myself. I'm just letting you in on the conversation.)

Truth be told, I don't have some magic formula for knowing when to walk away and when to keep plowing forward. All I can do is share what I've seen in three cities where I've been involved in church planting ... noting who stayed and who left. I also have my own stories. That's why I keep going back to calling. It's the rudder that guides us through the tumultuous seas of life and ministry. When you're living out your calling, you don't have to answer to anyone else. I'm not taking about being fiercely independent doing your own thing. What I mean is this ... let God guide and lead you. Walk closely with him. Make sure in the busyness and hubbub of ministry you're carving out daily time to hear from him and talk to him.

People all around you have an agenda for your life and church plant. Unfortunately, many of your network or denominational leaders have their livelihoods attached to how many churches they help get planted in their region. At times that means you're expendable. If you bail they have a lot more planters that they're recruiting to take your place. They'll say of you, "Remember that dude who tried planting in that neighborhood? What was his name again? Where is he?" I'm not saying you shouldn't seek help from older and wiser leaders. That's a must. But just be aware. Not everyone is acting out of the best motives.

Calling matters. A lot. It grounds you and gives you the strength to stay or go. I don't mean to turn this into an advertisement … but I write about this a lot more in *The Adventure of Vocation: Exploring the Contours of Calling, Identity, and Place*. I share a lot more stories that will hopefully give you more to think about. If you want a copy and money is tight, hit me up. I'm rooting for you.

AWKWRD

WHAT IF YOUR CHURCH PLANT ISN'T SUSTAINABLE IN 5 YEARS?

If there is a spiritual gift specifically given to church planters it's this ... naïveté. I mean that in a good way. How many embark on the church planting journey expecting failure? You know, the kinds of things we see across the church planting landscape ... mental health crises, broken marriages, financial ruin, fractured relationships, and moral failures just to name a few. Or that your church was stillborn. If you knew this going in would you still sign up? If you knew your church plant wouldn't "pop" by year five would you still plant it in the first place?

This past weekend I brought one of my sons on a road trip to explore rural Oregon. Recently I had read an article about the economic collapse of a certain timber town. Due to logging operations being owned by large corporations held by Wall Street suits they were able to sway lawmakers to get their taxes reduced to mere pennies. Once dependent on this essential tax base, it has left many communities financially dry when it came to funding schools, health services, and more. I wanted to find out.

With cameras in hand we left Portland. Sure enough, it was a tiny town, and we set out on foot to explore and take photos. There really wasn't much to see other than the evidences of poverty. On the way back we stopped at a different town to walk around their little downtown with the courthouse at its heart. Again, park, grab cameras, walk, take photos. Interestingly from the time we got out of the car to when we finished people were starting to gather for a Black Lives Matter (BLM) rally. Across the street was a contingent of counter-protestors. Several carried rifles. I saw lots of camo, cowboy hats, and trucker hats. Pick-up trucks were driving around with American flags streaming while "God Bless the U.S.A." was blasting out of their stereos. It was surreal.

I found it intriguing on many fronts. Observe. Take mental notes. Who was on the BLM side of the street? Who was on the other side? Were they wearing masks? Camo? As I had just finished writing my book *Intro to the City: 150 Observations to Understand the City* I've come to realize the power of observation. There is so much you can pick up and detect by simply watching … seeing … observing. Over time you note trends. You see patterns.

For almost twenty years I've been an observer in church planting. I've said that repeatedly now. The truth is, most church planters going into planting have the wonderful gift of naïveté. I know I did. Call it faith-filled naïveté. I'm not even using that word in a negative way nor as a slight. Naïveté is needed. Much needed. Why else would we sell homes, clean out retirements and savings, move across town or across country, and embark on an intensely spiritual, emotional, and mentally challenging adventure that is highly likely to fail?

Sure, many church planting leaders cite our updated and more robust church-planting assessments as proof of higher success rates. However, as I've pointed out, the elephant in the room is church planting as we know it is built on the planter's ability to gather Christians from other churches. So what have I noticed? Especially when it comes to the topic at hand?

You already know, because I've written about it repeatedly, is that most church plants are not sustainable by year five.

So now what?

Many church planters raised enough funding to at least get through those first five years. Their pluckiness, hubris, and naïveté tells them that they'll be "the one" who plants a thriving self-sustaining church within that timeframe. But since most of you won't, then what? What will you do?

If you're at that point more than likely you've not planned well for this day. That means you have really only one of two options … if you're still committed to the church. (A) You find a job. Maybe you only need a part-time job. Regardless of the source, you will need extra income to replace the declining outside support. If you're really good at fundraising, you'll woo your donors with tales of how people are simply "resistant to the gospel."

(No, they always have been. It's just that you're not as a big of deal as you first thought you were.)

Option (B) is to keep finding new supporters and more outside help and regale them with tales about your city's darkness. One church planter told me how all the unrest in Portland has boosted his fundraising among most of his supporters in the South. To them he is surely on the last frontier of global missions. (No, it's just Portland.)

I suppose there are a whole lot more than two options. You could leave altogether. You could leverage your church plant into landing a denominational gig (I did). Or you could merge with another church (which I actually highly recommend). Ultimately what you're weighing is whether or not you want to keep at church planting long-term. If you have twenty-five or thirty or forty people by year five how much larger do you think the church will you be by year ten? Are you content with a reality that says your church will never be large enough to pay your salary? If so, keep plugging away. Get that. If not? Well, you know what you need to do.

If you're yet to embark on your church planting journey, my encouragement to you is this … don't stop. Don't walk away. Just have a better plan. You probably won't hear any of this in your required denominational training. But if you knew this going in … if you were to somehow set aside some of your incredible gift of naïveté for just a moment … what would you do differently? I'm not saying, "Pack your bags and do something else. Church planting is nuts!" What I am saying is this … "Yes, you CAN do this. What's your plan? What's your plan for long-term sustainability for you and your family?"

The breaking point … where mental health crises, marriage troubles, and the like slip in … is often the result of not dealing with stress properly. What causes stress? Not measuring up to expectations as well as the painful reality that your funds will slowly diminish and any likelihood of a self-sustaining church plant is setting like the sun.

If you're already at the five-year point? I can't help you. If you're just starting off we can at least have a conversation or look at a course correction before you sail out from the harbor. If that's you, would you drop me an email? I'd love to talk.

CH 27

MOST CHURCH PLANTERS WILL NEED A CAREER OUTSIDE THEIR CHURCH

When we throw our lot into planting a church, we never ... or rarely ... think of doing anything other than planting a church. We assume that we'll simply and seamlessly transition from planting a new church to then pastoring this growing church full-time. However, for the majority of planters that day never comes. It's as if you're always stuck in the planting mode ... trying to get it off the ground. What is needed before venturing into planting is a plan and a strategy to develop a career outside of planting your church.

Unfortunately, for most of us, that's the farthest thing from our mind.

Here's the typical storyline. A person will leave his full-time job to venture into planting a new church. Maybe he's on staff at a church, maybe he worked in business or the non-profit world or tech or (fill in the blank). He assumes he needs to leave it all behind so he can jump into church planting with both feet. Often times that's what we're told needs to happen … or it's what we want. But we find scant biblical accounts that reinforce this.

Just this morning as I was reading Matthew 4 in my devotions I came across the account where Jesus calls his first disciples. "While walking by the Sea of Galilee, he saw two brothers, Simon (who is called Peter) and Andrew his brother, casting a net into the sea, for they were fishermen. And he said to them, 'Follow me, and I will make you fishers of men.' Immediately they left their nets and followed him." That passage resonated with me when I first ventured into paid ministry and church planting. Walk away. Leave everything behind. Push off from the shore of our old life … or our old career. Sacrifice all. And then something happens …

Our new church doesn't pop. We gotta get a job.

Panic ensues.

"Lord, I left it all. Like Peter, I left my nets and boats to follow you."

The challenge that is before us is applying specific texts to our own lives. That doesn't mean God doesn't use passages like these to nudge or draw us into a new ministry assignment. However, we also can point to (and need to point to) other New Testament passages where earning a living outside of ministry or church planting is actually quite normative. (Paul, for example).

So what does this mean going forward? I'm sorry but more than likely your church plant won't turn into the full-time gig you dreamed about. What that means is you need to go into church planting playing the long game with a career in mind other than church planting. Now mind you, I'm not here to tell you what that even is. Sure, through Intrepid we help church planters, pastors, and missionaries launch businesses and non-profits towards that end, but it's not the only way. Some of you will step into a ministry role with another organization or your denomination. You may step into real estate as an agent or a mortgage broker. Some will become junior high teachers. Others will transition back into tech. Others through the brokenness they experienced in church planting will step into counseling. The options are endless.

The point? You need a career. No, I'm not suggesting it as a backup plan. Instead, you need to make it *the* plan. Then if your church plant takes off beyond your wildest expectations you can pivot. If not, you'll panic as you make a hasty transition. You may find yourself walking away from your church completely. Worse yet, you'll step into some job or career you had no intention of pursuing and you're miserable.

You need a plan. You need a career. What will you choose?

WHY CURRENT FUNDING MODELS SHORT-CIRCUIT CHURCH PLANTING

In the church planting world are a lot of topics and issues that we dare not speak about ... out loud. Sometimes in hushed tones church planters will huddle together in the back corner of a coffee shop to speak of these things. But the hype machine known as church planting in North America keeps denominations and church planting organizations and networks from talking about some of the big elephants in the room. Which one in particular?

Funding.

It's the unspoken elephant in the room. It's like what happens when you gather together for holidays with your extended family. Your uncle … grandpa … is a bit racist. Everyone knows it. But after dinner sitting around the table he'll go off on one of his rants about "those people." One by one people will quietly get up from the table. No one wants to tell grandpa he's racist and ruin the cheer. But someone needs to.

It's that same reluctance which keeps us from confronting the obvious in church planting and funding. No one dares to mention in public … especially to the organizations who kick in funding … that our funding model is broken. The result is nothing short of competition and … dare I say … greed and envy among church planters. I bet you already know that. But no one wants to speak up. So we play along hoping someone else will. And we're stuck.

I'd make the case that our current funding policy breeds competition among planters for finite resources. Every semester I teach a university course called Interpersonal Communication. It is a blast of a class because we get into topics like intercultural communication, family of origin, and of course … conflict. Interestingly, a lack of resources is one of the sources of conflict. Elie Wiesel in *The Night*, his memoir of the Holocaust describes this horrific reality. Starving people would literally kill one another over a piece of bread. These had been well-regarded and upstanding citizens ... reduced to survival at all costs in the face of starvation.

I've seen a lot of ugliness in church planting (again, no one dares speak of it). I've felt the brunt of it. I've been hurt. My family has suffered. Much of it revolves around fighting over resources pitting church planters within the same denomination against each other jockeying over the same support churches who roll into town on these vision tours.

Tension noted. What is the solution?

Part-time church planting.

I just finished co-writing a book called *Part-Time Pastoring*. In one chapter I show how and why part-time pastoring or planting is the preferred future. Simply put, it's about resources. You see, if you go into church planting either working part-time or launching a startup or social enterprise at the same time you're not beholden to the petty infighting and tension that the current funding model creates. You're in it for the long term. You're not rushed. You're not forcing relationships and gathering Christians from other churches and calling it "church planting." You're able to send down deep roots and do the work of a true missionary.

How does that sound?

Pretty intoxicating if you ask me. I'd go for that kind of planting and funding model. That's why we do what we do at Intrepid. We believe in church planting as a missionary endeavor. We want to help you stay in it for the long term. To do so you need a funding model that can sustain you. This will also free you up to plant your lives and the gospel in lower-income communities that may never be able to support a full-time pastor / planter. But that's OK … that's not why you are planting there in the first place.

CH 29

"TALK TO ME WHEN YOU'VE RUN OUT OF MONEY"

In the university classroom this semester I did something I hadn't done before. I begin every class with a quote pertinent to the subject I'm teaching on. If it's on bicycles, equity, and race then all the quotes pertain to those subjects. If it's on calling, vocation, spirituality, and character then most quotes explore the parameters of the kind of life we ought to live, the adventure, and leaning into how we're wired and gifted. I'm always on the hunt for a good quote and I regularly search for them. They come from books and movies and online searches. I display them on the screen and we talk.

One of my favorite is the well-known Mike Tyson one that goes, "Everyone has a plan 'till they get punched in the mouth." That is applicable in more areas of life than we'd like to admit. Not too long ago I was at a church planting event, a roundtable of sorts. Featured were church planters and those who've done well at raising funds exclusively for planting. It's church planting bliss. I applaud them.

I couldn't help but think of all of the other planters in the room. I thought, "Talk to me when you've run out of funding." Those with ample support are going all-out on church planting. Then their funding runs out ... and panic. They've come to a crossroads. I've seen many such church planters' crossroads. I've hit it too. It's where you decide ... (A) keep going regardless which means getting a job, (B) keep trying like mad to raise more funds by convincing supporters that the plant is almost ready to take off, (C) start sending your resume out to other churches and ministries, or (D) start a business or non-profit.

Very few church planters avoid that crossroads. No one anticipates it. We all assume that we'll be the ones to actually "make it." One of my pleas through Intrepid is for church planters to begin this conversation even before they begin planting. Make it part of your strategy from the outset rather than hitting the panic button when your plans didn't work out. However, most of us are stubborn and naive. I know I am. That's actually a great combination of traits. If we were to look at planting rationally and realistically very few of us would ever venture into it because of all the risks and uncertainties involved.

I'm not trying to be critical of planting. I just know planters. Would I have ever considered something like Intrepid when I first ventured into planting? No way. I was convinced I would be the anomaly that would actually succeed. I was wrong so I got a job and worked bivocationally. And I LOVED it. It changed my life. I tell people that if I had been a good fundraiser and successful church planter there'd be no Intrepid. It was born out of my own failures and shortcomings. My hope now is to help you avoid some of the same.

The bottom line is there are lots of ways to fund church planting, missionary endeavors, and community development initiatives. Starting a new venture, whether a business or non-profit, is simply one way.

AWKWRD

CH 30

PASTORS ARE CHOOSING THE WRONG PLATFORM: HOW TO CHOOSE THE RIGHT ONE

I'm on social media just as much as the next person, if not more. I manage six different accounts including my own. I teach an undergrad course on it. Whether related to Intrepid, my personal account, coffee, academia, or urban studies I spend a lot of time on social media. Not as much time perusing feeds as I am posting and interacting. I see a lot of accounts and profiles. I also see a lot of social media accounts and profiles of pastors and church planters. Too many. It's painful to watch. I feel like that person who comes upon a car crash. You know you shouldn't look, but you can't help it. That's how I feel about the innumerable social profiles I see from churches, church plants, pastors, and church planters.

In today's digital economy the name of the game is building your platform and capitalizing (or monetizing) off it. I get that. I too wrestle with that tension. Since part of my life revolves around academia I am most certainly trying to promote my writings and books through a variety of platforms. I'm not crying foul. But what I will say is this ... if ministry is your focus, whether via a church or church planting, then building your personal platform is not the way to go. Don't get me wrong. It's great if you're about connecting with other Christians in your community and wooing them to your church. But if it's about connecting the ninety-to-ninety-five percent "others" who'd never set foot inside one of your worship gatherings then your supposed platform is self-promotional at best.

Why?

I love spending time in the classroom everyday with university students, particularly those who didn't grow up in church. They have no idea who the latest Christian celebrities are. They think

Hillsong is about that scene in *The Sound of Music* when people are, well, singing in the hills. They don't know the latest celebrity pastors in their expensive shoes and Gucci belts. They are wonderfully unaware that such a world even exists. So young pastor or church planter, when you try to build your platform using that same template, it is certain to land with a hollow thud. Only a small slice of church people even know that. Everyone else has no idea. The questions are … what kind of platform are you trying to build? And who are you trying to connect with?

You're building the wrong platform.

At Intrepid we're all about helping you establish and build a platform to connect with people in your community who don't get or like church. It looks like a new business or non-profit. A social enterprise. Why is this important?

If you walk into a social circle with your I'm-an-awesome-preacher-pastor-platform people will look at you oddly. It doesn't resonate nor connect with the rest of culture. On the other hand, if your platform is a new artisan bakery, non-profit tutoring program, bike repair shop, coworking space, the new chapter of a trail-building organization, and so on then people will get you. They'll get you for you.

They won't know that you know how to preach verse-by-verse in the ESV and like to read and quote dead theologians. All they will know is, "Hey, you're that dude who fixed my daughter's bike." Or, "Hey, you run that new bakery. I LOVE your gluten free muffins!"

See the difference?

If we spent more time building these kinds of platforms rather than our own we would see the gospel demonstrated more in our communities and give people the opportunity to hear the good news of a Savior who left his heavenly platform, came to earth to serve (not to be served), and to give his life as a ransom for our sins. All it takes is a willingness to set yourself apart for the sake of others and start a business or non-profit.

CH 31

WHY CHURCH PLANTING IS A HORRIBLE INVESTMENT

I've changed a lot over the last twenty years. Most notably, I've changed in how I view church planting. In particular, about how we fund church planting. I think it's a horrible investment.

Now it's time for the fine print or the warning label. You know, like the ones you see on every prescription bottle. "Side-effects may include: suicidal ideation, paralysis, and even death." Here's my warning label or fine print … things that need to be said before we proceed any further:

I believe in church planting. I believe in church planters.

I simply think we have a flawed system in how we go about planting churches in North America. It breeds competition among planters for scarce resources. It elevates the very tiny few who actually make it. Those who don't or can't make it are simply tossed aside without second thought. You know … collateral damage. Ministry casualties. The price to be paid.

Many church planters "sell the farm," move across the country, and are able to pry a tiny bit of funds can from denominations and donors. Sure, some do it well and are living like church planting kings. These are the one-percenters of the church planting world. But for most? After five years their funds will have mostly dried up, they will be working bivocationally in some career they don't really care for, and feel stuck. You can't uproot and leave because then you will feel even more like a failure. You'll remember the $200,000, $300,000, or $750,000 invested in you and your church plant over those years. Even though your supporters are disappointed their investment didn't result in a church that's exploding with growth (even if it is mostly transfer growth), you don't want to take your ailing church off life support and watch it die. That would be too traumatic for you and your donors.

So what do you do?

That's why I say that church planting is a horrible investment. Because it is. These stories are not anomalies. They are reality. They reflect the typical storyline in church planting. The problem though is your denomination or church planting organization never tells you those stories. Their leaders need to keep their jobs, pay their bills, and save for retirement. They're going to keep doing what they can to crank out new church plants knowing that once in a while one may stick. And if that's not you then you simply are expendable. Collateral damage. These are the truths no one will tell you other than other planters who're years ahead of you.

So ... if church planting is a horrible investment then why am I involved? I'll say it gain ... I believe in church planting. I believe in church planters. We simply need a shift in how we go about the process.

If you've followed me and Intrepid for any length of time you know about my love for planters and planting. All I'm doing is advocating for a different way to get you to the same destination. And what is that destination? To see you plant a church, stay rooted long-term, be self-sustainable, and find creative ways to love your neighborhood, district, town, or city.

How?

By starting a business or non-profit that create alternate income streams that not only keep you rooted long-term in place, they become the very strategy you use to plant your church AND give back to the city you love.

Sounds too easy?

Well, that's because it isn't.

Startups are hard. But so is church planting. If you were looking for the easy route you wouldn't be interested in church planting in the first place. I just want to help you succeed long-term.

CH 32

WHAT YOU NEED TO KNOW ABOUT BIVOCATIONAL CHURCH PLANTING GOING IN

This past week brought about a convergence of conversations about the realities of church planting that are evident in cities (and rural communities) across the country. Not that these realities are even new or noteworthy, but how they landed together at the same time.

Last week I had coffee with a friend who's a church planter. We've both been in Portland now long enough to have seen the tide carry new church planters into the city and to watch mortified as the tide swept most of them back out to sea. One by one we talked about all of the planters we know who've already come and gone over the past six-to-eight years. That's not that long a time frame.

The reasons why they left are mixed. Any time I've met with a church planter who was contemplating leaving I've always tried to be supportive and encouraging. I want what's best for them and their family. Usually at that point they need a change or a reprieve.

Then I had two conversations with planters in two separate cities who were both facing the same struggles within their denomination. There's not much of a family or brotherhood among the planters since the system is set up to breed competition. There's a revolving door of vision tours where potential partner churches and their pastors are paraded all over the city. They're oversold the city's "darkness," and then they meet the prospective church planters.

Each planter is most often desperately hoping and praying to be able to "land" another partner. New partners equal more money even if it means having to put up with annoying mission teams from their churches. Both planters I talked with admitted their frustration with the "system" but since they're part of it they don't know what else to do. But since they're both well-funded they also recognize the benefits.

Another layer or thread to these interconnected conversations is the looming reality that planters are facing, have faced, or will face soon. Here's how it works ... Unless you're a "one-percenter" church planter with strong funding you're either already bivocational, transitioning into bivocational work, or are contemplating when to seriously consider making that leap. For most church planters it's not a matter of if but when.

The only difference between them and the well-funded planters is the timeline. Sooner or later they will all have to make that transition.

While I advocate, teach on, and champion bivocational church planting it's not the secret silver bullet that will slay the soul-sucking funding vampire. For some? For sure! For others, it means stepping into an industry or field for which they've been ill-equipped, nor educated, or trained. Many of those with an MDiv are picking up jobs that don't require even a Bachelor's degree to do.

That said, bivocational church planting, while it is challenging, is still worth it. That's assuming you're passionate and energized about planting. What's even more helpful is if you also feel that way about your "other" job, whether you step into a job or career on the side or whether you've gone through our coaching and are launching a new business or non-profit from scratch.

Here's what you need to know going in ... it's a lot of work. You may fail. You may succeed. You simply won't know until you try.

Just this morning I was reading through Malcom Gladwell's *Outliers* in preparation for a new course I'll soon begin teaching. I was riveted. Gladwell brilliantly wove the story of the plight of different immigrant groups landing in New York City at around the turn of the twentieth century. Many who had a previous skillset, particularly in the garment industry, found they could make a good run at it in their new home. As Gladwell writes, "autonomy, complexity, and a connection between effort and reward—are, most people agree, the three qualities that work has to have if it is to be satisfying. It is not how much money we make that ultimately makes us happy between nine and five. It's whether our work fulfills us"[1]

Many were willing to work insanely long and difficult hours, but why? Because it was meaningful.

---

[1] Gladwell, *Outliers*, 149-150.

It wasn't mundane. They were entrepreneurial in the truest sense. Lots of risk. No guarantees they'd succeed. Similarly, those who enter bivocational work are doing so because they have a calling—a compulsion—to do this. No guarantees. It's downright terrifying. You may not always be able to pay the bills. You may not be able to afford those Instagram-worthy vacations your friends on staff at the big churches take. But you don't care. You're invigorated by the possibilities. You see opportunities where others may see obstacles.

Again, what do you need to know going in? Simply put ... you more than likely won't "make it." I hear all time about church planters' survivability and success rates. As if that will somehow encourage someone to step into planting churches. I think those numbers are skewed. Based on my experiences, I can tell you that it's actually rare for a church plant to make it. Yes, I said rare.

That's why we need to take this bivocational conversation seriously. As I always contend ... if you as the planter are sustainable (however you can make that happen) then your church will be sustainable. This is certainly not doom and gloom. Far from it. This is good news! Church planting is hard! Bivocational church planting is more difficult in terms of juggling your two jobs. But just like the Jewish immigrants from rural Poland who landed in New York City in 1889 you have the skillset needed to thrive. As they say … high risk, high reward. I'm pulling for you. It is a privilege to do what we do.

CH 33

FINDING SUCCESS IN A RESULTS-DRIVEN MINISTRY WORLD

Every church planter wants one thing and only one thing … success. But what is "success"? If every church planter is plagued by this word, is measured up against this word, and their entire funding and livelihood is tied to it then it would be prudent for them to find it and capitalize on it. But we have a problem …

A big problem.

What is success?

Go ahead and cite innumerable verses from the New Testament on what success in church planting should look like. Asked and answered, right? The problem is your denomination, donors, and support churches aren't looking at those verses, metrics, or definitions. They only are interested in ensuring a good return on their investment. You're like a stock that they invested in. And you better be Apple and not Blockbuster.

So you're left with a dilemma.

Play the game and hope you can deliver at least a marginally "profitable" stock. Or, stay true to your convictions and go after what you know to be true biblical "success" that is not tied to hype, false promises, and living under the crushing weight of other peoples' expectations. About twelve years ago I decided to stop playing this game. I'm not a stock. Besides, I'm not very good at trying to be like one. Instead, I began asking myself, "If I were a missionary and not a church planter, what would I do?"

That changed everything.

Funny thing, though, is how we play with terms. I began jettisoning what a church planter "should" do and started acting like what a missionary "over there" does. Immediately my pace slowed down. I got off the treadmill. There was no rat race to participate in. I took the long-term approach. I still do. I started pursuing other interests and passions that are part of who I am. Ironically, the more I do that the more ministry opportunities I have that were never afforded me as a "normal" church planter. In fact, I share the good news of the Kingdom so much that I don't even think about it or keep track. There are no monthly reports to fill out and boxes to check (and lie about so I wouldn't lose my funding).

I've become the kind of missionary I dreamed about. And here's the beauty of it … I'm not living in the volatile Wall Street-like world where "success" is measured by how many people show up on a Sunday morning or whether or not my core group is growing. Trust me, I'm more passionate about evangelism and discipleship than ever before, but as a missionary I simply go about it in a way that's not trying to appease donors and support-churches.

The key to finding success in a results-driven ministry world is simply this … stop playing the game. Get off the treadmill. But there's a catch. To do so means you need a livelihood outside of church planting. Until you do you'll forever continue playing the game. Sure, a few do it well and catch lightning in a bottle. But for every one of those there are twenty-to-thirty other church planters who're spectacularly "mediocre." That's OK, because I am too. I like it that way.

That's why I started Intrepid … to focus on people and places church planters rarely care about and do so in a way that is sustainable long-term. Would you join me?

CH 34

WHERE ARE YOU GOING TO PLANT A CHURCH? IN PLACES YOU LIKE OR IN PLACES OF NEED?

Every church planter faces a dilemma. It becomes a moral dilemma if they actually take time to reflect on the ramifications. The dilemma is ... Where should I plant a church? I've given more thought and researched no other topic in church planting than this one. In the economics world this is called site selection and every business wrestles with this. Where's the best place to put in a new (insert the kind of business here). Ultimately, the goal is to maximize what the business is about ...

whether it's a distribution center, a pub, a bike shop, a law office, a new hospital, or whatever.

So how does one decide on where to plant a church?

Also, what should be the most influential factors? Ultimately, what wins out?

I love to explore the city on my bike as I've already shared. It's my ticket to adventure. It is also my tool to see and begin to understand various neighborhoods up-close and personal. It's an exercise (pun intended) in on-the-ground demographic research. For example, if I were to start my bike ride in the Pearl District in the heart of Portland what would I see? Lots of nice cars, expensive restaurants, and well-dressed people on the sidewalks and hanging out in parks. This is where the Instagram influencers hang out. However, the farther I pedal away from the city center I observe as the scenery changes before me.

Portland is America's largest "white city." But once you leave the predominantly white city center, block by block the demographics shift right before your eyes. You notice how the kinds of businesses and housing change. I can point to a number of parks where I see more people of color whether on the sidewalks or walking in and out of businesses.

I'm literally watching the city change as I ride by. That's why I affectionately call this the "Other Portland."

Yet interestingly, it seems the bulk of the church planting is in the city center. I think a fun research project would be juxtaposing coffee shops (or coffee roasters) with church plants. My hypothesis is that the higher concentration of new hip coffee shops runs on parallel tracks with the higher concentration of new churches. Why? Because coffee shops are either a harbinger of a neighborhood's gentrification or that a saturation of them reveals it's already gentrified. In other words, the neighborhoods with these coffee shops and new churches are viewed as having a lot of curb appeal.

Conversely, the farther out from the city center I pedal from the city center the fewer coffee shops I see other than a drive-through Starbucks or Dutch Brothers. What does that tell us? Lots.

I've wondered why the number one criterion for most church planters revolves around this whole livability conversation. Whether we're talking about a hip urban neighborhood or a family-friendly suburb with top-rated schools it seems the priority becomes livability and aesthetic appeal. That brings up the questions I asked in the title of this chapter ... Where are you going to plant a church? In places you like or in places of need?

I used to be all-in on church planting in the heart of the city. Back then in many cities it was neglected and overlooked as the locus of church planting endeavors. Most planters at that time were opting for the suburbs. Then something magical happened. Gentrification. That meant the urban core became "livable" ... cool, hip, desirable, and ready to recolonize (after whites had fled the city centers decades earlier).

As one who teaches university-level urban studies courses I understand neighborhood succession over decades and even centuries as populations come and go. Cities are constantly in flux. I get that. However, church planting as a trend seems to follow the front edge of development or redevelopment, from the suburban frontier as new developments continue to pop up to the urban core as neighborhoods are "revitalized" (as if people weren't already living there, running businesses, and worshipping in churches).

Church planter, which are you going to choose? Will you choose a place or part of the city where you've always dreamed of living (which would also be a great lifestyle accessory) or will you choose a place in need? (I have deliberately not defined "need.") Whichever you choose I won't fault you. I just want to have a conversation, ask questions, probe, and get you thinking a little more on this topic.

If you want to process this more hit me up. I'd love to be a listening ear and a sounding board.

AWKWRD

CH 35

MAINSTREAM OR FRINGE: WE NEED VOICES FROM THE MARGINS

I'm not embarrassed to admit this, but for the most part years ago I stopped reading books related to ministry, and in particular church planting. Once in a while I do, but mostly I steer away. That's because too often there's little new or newsworthy out there. It's kind of like boy bands …

The phenomenon of boy bands is a tried and true and very successful music franchise and genre. It's more than having an all-male cast of singers. There's also a certain sound, a vibe, and an aura about boy bands. One band called *New Edition* had its start in the late 70s and became popular in the early 80s. They were an all-black group that I grew up listening to (and still listen to today). In a similar vein was *Boyz II Men*. *New Kids on the Block* tweaked the genre with an all-white cast. Nonetheless, whether we're talking about *N'Sync*, *Backstreet Boys*, *98 Degrees*, or *BTS* today I think we can agree there's a certain sound and vibe to it all. It's also crazy popular.

Does the popularity of the boy band era mean the music or quality is subpar? Maybe musically it's not the best, but vocally many would contend they have incredible talent (*Boyz II Men*? Come on. Crazy talented.) Sure, after a while many of them sound eerily similar. That's not including the dozens if not hundreds of knock-offs who also sound pretty much the same. Even the Christian music industry in the late 90s tried jumping into the scene.

The pushback on the genre is the lack of creativity which no one would say was the case with the early pioneers. Since those early days it seems every boy band has sounded the same.

The same is true in books on ministry and church planting. After a while they all start to sound as predictable as another boy band with the same beat and generic lyrics. Too often these books look back to some ministry success that even most of those involved were surprised that it had actually taken off. Publishers are are like record labels seeking out and signing the next hot boy band in hopes they take off and make them a lot of money. It's the same with books by trendy authors on ministry or church planting books that get cranked out ... with the same beat and lyrics.

The painful reality though is that most often innovation and new ideas come from the margins ... not the mainstream. What I mean is that innovation at the margins comes two sources: (A) cross-pollination with other subjects or disciplines and (B) marginalized or minority voices. Let me unpack these a little more ...

Fusions offer one source of innovation. There's a lot of creativity that comes from studying other subjects and disciplines. What happens if you pair church planting with urban studies or with digital media or with community development or with startups or with ... you get the point. I also intentionally dropped in some disciplines that are influential to Intrepid. Innovation happens when we merge subjects and disciplines. It's not always neat and tidy. Sometimes things can be taken too far ... like American evangelicalism's love affair with the business world and the CEO model of leadership. All we have to do is note how many pastors continue to be removed because of running roughshod over their staff and church members. Fusions are good, but they should be vetted.

The other source of innovation comes from marginalized and minority voices. I'm talking about truly left-off-the-radar voices and leaders. Those without a platform. They probably don't even have social media. Instead they're laboring away in ministry because of a deep sense of conviction and calling rather than seeing it as a great career move. Just this past week in class I had to remind students that yes, even ministry can be quite lucrative ... one can make crazy money in ministry. Marginalized leaders have much to teach us because they serve God not expecting anything in return ... most often that also means not receiving a paycheck to plant and lead churches. They have much wisdom.

In terms of minority voices I have two thoughts in mind ... (A) minority in terms of ethnicity and (B) minority in terms of global status. We need to draw inspiration from a whole variety of voices and perspectives that are not our own. That could be as basic as an ethnicity or a nationality that are not our own. Are you listening to voices from other countries and continents? Are you drawing from the wells of other theological camps? That doesn't mean you have to agree with everything they say since every camp has its blind spots. But we need to humbly acknowledge and learn from the voices of the global church.

Lastly, in terms of global status, what are we learning from leaders and practitioners who're doing ministry in challenging places? Mind you, most places in the world make Portland look like the Bible Belt. We need to hear from leaders who're laboring in fields where there is little to no harvest. How do they do it? How do they stick it out year after year with little to nothing to show for it? I want to hear those voices.

Listen, there's nothing wrong with the mainstream. It's mainstream for a reason. It's popular. But like boy bands, popularity doesn't always equal excellence. Because something is popular in the ministry world doesn't mean we need to consume it. Unfortunately, this is par for the course in church planting. Almost every church planter seeks to "launch big" which is code for hoping to be the next big deal … and get a book deal from a big publisher. But what if church planting is more than a popularity contest? If the answer is yes, then we need to turn to the margins to draw fresh inspiration.

CH 36

PLANTING CHURCHES IN A MAJORITY CULTURE SYSTEM

It's not debatable that church planting systems in the U.S. overwhelmingly favor white church planters who're planting churches in white neighborhoods. Having now spent nearly two decades as a participant and observer, I am confident that this is a fact. Truth be told, it is one of the reasons why I started Intrepid. But first, a story ...

A number of years ago I participated in a vision tour in Montréal, Canada. To this day it is still one of my favorite cities. The idea of the tour was simple ...

gather a group of large church pastors from the American South, get them to Montréal, show them around the city, feed them great food (I gladly had poutine a number of times), and connect them with church planters in hopes that these churches would become major supporters.

One night at dinner all of the church planters were introduced. Over the next few days that was followed up by visiting the different sites where these church planters were hoping to start new churches. I'll never forget one church planter in particular. Most (not all) of the others were white, but he was a black African from francophone Africa. I watched the big-church pastors fawn over all the church planters ... except him. They received all of the love and attention. I'm not even sure this black church planter left the vision tour with any supporters. This was another "a-ha" moment for me when I saw again how the system is rigged. It favors the one (white) and not the many (minorities). That's why I came up with the idea or motif that these vision tours are like runway fashion shows. Let me explain ...

There is one goal and one goal alone for these kinds of vision tours ... to get outside churches to support and be involved in church planting. It's actually a good idea. I'm in favor. However, and this is where the fashion show analogy comes in, the sexier the church planter (or hip and cooler) and the better they are at communicating their vision of their hip church in a hip and exciting neighborhood the more likely that a large church will become a supporter. Thus the fashion show rewards the good looking (white) church planter. Most often the support-church pastors are white so they automatically "get" white culture and understand what the predominantly white planters are trying to do, start, and become.

Too often, I've watched minority church planters … black, Hispanic, Filipino, and others not catch the eye of these support churches. Why? Because these pastors most often don't have a framework for doing ministry outside of majority culture nor in the margins. This black church planter in Montréal was a mere janitor. Hardly the candidate that a large (white) church from the South would want to drop tens or hundreds of thousands of dollars on. But they would gladly throw it at the well-coiffed white church planter who plans to "launch big."

This vision tour was really nothing more than a fashion show. The black planter was barely allowed to be in the room let alone get invited to walk the runway. I've watched Hispanic church planters who are reaching agricultural workers receive the same treatment.

And so they move on ... with the calling that God has placed on their lives ... with or without outside help or support. That's why so many minority planters are bivocational. Not because it's hip and trendy. It's a stark reality compared to the many white church planters I know who have so much support they roll into their cities with years and years of funding guaranteed, buying expensive homes, taking lots of vacations, and not even working a forty-hour week. For many of the other planters not living the dream as a majority culture church planter they're working 40-60 hours a week AND THEN planting a church on top of it.

Yes, I know I'm speaking in broad generalities and this isn't the case 100 percent of the time. However, there is little doubt that church planting in the U.S. favors the majority culture ... even though it won't be long before what we label the "majority" and the "minority" will be flipped around. I look forward to that day. Unfortunately, until then this is the reality in church planting. It is the reality in terms of the missionaries we send abroad as they too are predominantly white.

My heart for starting Intrepid is to advocate for the margins ... the overlooked ... the non-majority culture ... places and people left out of most church planting strategies. Am I the only one? Not by a long shot. Am I there yet? Hardly. Do I have blind-spots? Too many to count. I recognize I too am part of the majority culture ... white, educated, etc. I recognize too that Intrepid attracts more people who look like me than don't. I long to correct this imbalance someday. The sooner the better.

Do I have the answer? No. Have I crafted a document to submit to all denominations and church planting organizations that addresses this issue? No. But for me the first step was to at least point out these realities. While they are nothing new, my hope is we can correct this, whether we're talking church planting in North America or international missions. Something needs to change.

CH 37

WHERE DID THE FRONTIER GO?

If you've followed Intrepid for any length of time you will know that this notion of frontiers is pivotal and even formative for me. Maybe because I classify Intrepid as somewhat a missions organization (or missions training ministry) I'm constantly thinking about not only frontiers, but in particular the frontier of missions.

That's a moving target.

I'm getting ready to teach an undergrad course basically on global missions. We'll explore contemporary pressing issues affecting global missions. To prepare, I've binge-read tons of books.

As we highlight various countries it's striking to be reminded that the global church is quite robust. Strong. Rapidly expanding. God is clearly at work all over the world. In fact, there are many countries that have been targeted by North American missions that actually have a very large Christian population. Some of these same countries are also now mission-sending powerhouses.

So what does this have to do with frontiers?

Everything.

It's only natural for those of us born and raised in North America to view and interpret the world we live in through the geo-political lens of being an American or a Canadian. Also, do you see what I just did? It's myopic to assume that "North America" comprises only the U.S. and Canada, when in fact it also includes Mexico, Costa Rica, Haiti, Panama, and more. So let me revise that … "It's only natural for those of us born and raised in the U.S. to view and interpret the world we live in through the geo-political lens of being an American." We don't mean to, but we assume cultural superiority as Americans, right? I mean, we have Kanye, Lebron, the NFL, and apple pie. But we also have significant social unrest, imbedded systemic racism, and a whole slew of human rights violations.

So why and how do so many assume that the frontier of missions is still "somewhere out there?" Somewhere beyond the borders of the United States. We have thousands of youth groups swooping down on Mexico or Guatemala to build houses or put on backyard Bible clubs. They go with good intentions ... but why do they go at all? We fail to realize that these countries have their own seminaries, megachurches, celebrity pastors, and everything else the American church has.

What if I told you the frontier was actually right here under our noses? Now before you load up your youth group in your church's egg-white 15-passenger van with a trailer full of low-budget sports equipment, let me explain. I'm more convinced than ever that our mission frontier is right here. Before us. Both urban and rural. You don't even need a passport to get there.

Now, I'm not being dismissive of those who go oversees for mission work. Nor am I being dismissive of the fact there are still plenty of places and people in the world in need of outsiders to bring and live out the gospel. But the need for missions within the U.S. really hit home a few years ago when I was emailing the director of a rural church planting organization. He said, "Sean, mission organizations are still sending missionaries to countries with a lot higher Christian population than many rural counties throughout the Western United States." With our obsession with the *there* it appears we have overlooked the *here*. Especially when the *here* has changed dramatically.

Once in a while I'm tempted to say, "We need to stop sending missionaries." Or, "Please, church planters, stay home. Yes, your home town isn't as cool as Portland, but they need you more than Portland does. Stay home." (I'm being tongue-in-cheek … maybe.)

I have already interacted with several students who'll be in my class. I know they're at school getting a degree so they can graduate and "go on the mission field." While I won't steer them away from going overseas, instead what I hope to do is expand their thinking. It's stuff we already know. You're already on the mission field. Is that a cliché? Probably. But it's more real to me than ever before.

Of all of the things I am, have been involved in, and am currently doing I self-identity predominantly as this. A missionary. No, I don't broadcast it. It's not on a business card. It's not on my Instagram bio. But at my core I am a missionary (an ambassador of Christ, one who's been sent). Does that mean I get "paid" to be one? No, but that's a different conversation for another day. Yet oddly enough, most often when we talk about "missionaries" or "missions" then all of a sudden the conversation turns to geography. Why is there a place for missions out there and not here?

Sure, Portland has its share of megachurches, well-known ministries, and celebrity pastors. But as far as those outside of the Christian bubble are concerned they don't even exist. Ninety-five to ninety-seven percent or more of Portland have never heard of them. Yet church planters all still focus on and target that same tiny demographic of Bible-believing Christians. In other words, why do I need to go somewhere else to be a missionary? All I have to do is walk outside my door.

I admit I've asked more than answered. I've brought up more points than clarified. I suspect you know what I'm saying and what I'm not saying. One of my roles with Intrepid is to raise up and train a new generation of missionaries. The only difference between them and those from other missions organization is that they're missionaries here.[1]

You in?

---

[1] Also keep in mind we work with missionaries and leaders from other countries as well. We've worked and will always work with individuals, ministries, and organizations mobilizing and sending people all over the world.

CH 38

YOU WILL BE MISUNDERSTOOD

The longer I coach and meet with church planters the clearer I see the unfortunate games that we play in ministry. In particular, one that I often see played out is related to geography. The rules of this game are simple ... they go like this:

For a church planter serving anywhere outside your home country everything is on the table when it comes to strategy and methodology. Innovation and creativity are the name of the game. But for that same person with the same passion to reach people within their home country then the rules change ... dramatically. All of a sudden, most strategies and methodologies get taken off the table. What is left is usually someone else's "tried and true" way to plant a church and do ministry.

Recently I met with a church planter who told me of a conversation he had had a couple years ago with his denomination. As part of his church planting strategy he wanted to launch a creative startup. Why? To build something that will fund him long-term. But more importantly, the group of people he wanted to serve (and is serving) are an unreached / under-reached cultural tribe or subculture. Almost no other planter is even thinking about them let alone connecting with them. But the real source of the tension he felt was how his denomination viewed him. They don't know what box or category to put him in.

Mind you, if he was doing this in Spain, South Africa, or India or anywhere outside the U.S., his strategies and methodologies would receive nothing but praise and applause. But since he's not spending fifteen hours a week in sermon prep his denomination is not sure if he should receive his funding. (They literally told that to him.)

Conversely, take the same planter with the same strategy and put him in Madrid or Barcelona and we'd be chiding him if he *did* spend 15 hours a week in sermon prep. We'd encourage him to get away from that. To be more incarnational ... in the people ... among the people. But here? Well, he was reprimanded for not "acting like a real church planter."

If you want to move in this direction and do what you believe to be best to reach the people you want to reach then know it comes with a warning label ... you WILL be misunderstood. People won't get what you're doing. They'll tell you that what you're doing is wrong or bad strategizing. You're doing what it takes to go after people you love dearly. Do that over there? Absolutely! But here? Well, you're a bit odd. You will be misunderstood.

Your sending church most often won't get you. Your denomination won't get you either. Many of your donors won't get you. Many of your peers won't get you. Instead, funding will be channeled away from you to the other church planters in your city who're trying to "launch big" and are holding preview services (for other Christians ... who else shows up to those things?). You will be misunderstood.

You're at a crossroads.

I see it all the time with church planters. Which direction to pursue? Your heart yearns to connect with people who have zero interest in worship gatherings regardless of how trendy they are. So you dream of ways to connect with these overlooked people. That involves moving into a "domestic missionary" mode rather than a "church planter" mode. But that is often a lonely path ... that doesn't get nearly the support that other planters receive. At this crossroads you're faced with choosing which to go ... pursue your heart and lose out on a lot of funding ... or reluctantly slide into the "tried and true" way of church planting that promises ample funding and lots of nods of approval.

CH 39

CALLING ALL MISFITS

Some call them misfits, I call them intrepid adventurers. Either way they're misunderstood and maligned. Swimming upstream of conventional ministry or church planting wisdom is to invite skepticism and resistance from your leaders and peers. "You can't plant that way." "You're supposed to do it like this." But what if "this" isn't you? What if for some glorious reason you're an outlier … a disruptor … a creative … a misfit? Intrepid is for you.

Because of our focus most often those who're drawn here are more on the creative or misfit end of the spectrum. Almost always they share stories of pain and misunderstanding. "When I shared with my senior pastor that I think God is calling me to plant he fired me." "I wanted to move to where we're planting and get a job so I could take time to get to know the people." "Launching a startup isn't a strategy on top of church planting … it is our church planting strategy." "I don't want to be dependent upon supporters for my church plant."

While there's nothing new or noteworthy in those statements, they reveal a rift in how we approach church planting. Somehow there's the "right way" and there's the "wrong way." Ah yes, the "right way" is alive and well. Since I'm on social media every day throughout the day for Intrepid I see this "right way" at work. Social media feeds of church plants are full of trendy worship gatherings with their Hillsong-look-alike bands and trendy young pastor. They usually have their photography and Lightroom presets dialed. There are A LOT of great photos of the well-coiffed pastor preaching … whether in-person or from his trendy cool living room. Perusing social media reveals what to them church planting should look like.

But what if that isn't you? What if your goal and ambition isn't to reach other trendy Christians? What if you actually want to go to the least and the last ... the ... overlooked, the marginalized, the forgotten? There's nothing wrong with church planters who look good. May their ministries be blessed. But what if you're inclined to swim upstream? Against the flow. Against the conventional wisdom?

I'm calling all misfits. The misunderstood. The maligned. Those who don't check all the boxes. Those who actually think launching a social enterprise while church planting is your preferred future. It doesn't mean you won't have a worship gathering. It doesn't mean you won't have nice things. But your focus is not to simply put on trendy worship gatherings for trendy people. You see yourself more as a missionary with a burning desire for those who have no interest in trendy worship services. Or really worship of any kind. In order to connect with those it'll take intentionally going to where they are ... the highways and byways of society that most church planters avoid.

Are you in? Let's do this. Together.

BIBLIOGRAPHY

Gladwell, Malcolm. *Outliers: The Story of Success.* New York: Back Bay, 2011.

Heying, Charles. *Brew to Bikes: Portland's Artisan Economy.* Portland: Ooligan, 2010.

Hunter, George G. *The Celtic Way of Evangelism: How Christianity Can Reach the West ... Again.* Nashville: Abingdon, 2010.

Lipschultz, Jeremy. *Social Media Measurement and Management.* New York: Routledge, 2020.

Mile, Jason. *Instagram Power: Build Your Brand and Reach More Customers with Visual Influence.* New York: McGraw-Hill, 2019.

Payne, J.D. "Mission and Church Planting." In *Theology and Practice of Mission: God, the Church, and the Nations*, edited by Bruce Riley Ashford, 200-210. Nashville: B&H Academic, 2011.

Wright, Christopher J.H. *The Mission of God's People: A Biblical Theology of the Church's Mission.* Grand Rapids: Zondervan Academic, 2010.

AUTHOR

Sean Benesh lives in the Portland, Oregon and is a professor, author, and leads an organization called Intrepid. He is the author of *Through Barren Wastelands: In Search of Explorers, Pioneers, Misfits, and the Apostolic Imagination* and over twenty other books related to church planting, social entrepreneurship, and the city.